D0915455

WASHED ASHORE

WASHED ASHORE

Family, Fatherhood, and Finding Home
on Martha's Vineyard

A Memoir

BILL EVILLE

June 2023

Maria,

From film to now - love to
Reconnect on our journeys.

Bill E.

Published in 2023 by

GODINE

Boston, Massachusetts

LIBRARY OF CONGRESS CONTROL NUMBER 2022950258
ISBN 978-1-56792-738-2

First Printing, 2023
Printed in the United States of America

To Cathlin, Hardy, and Pickle

"It is important to tell at least from time to time the secret of who we truly and fully are— even if we tell it only to ourselves—because otherwise we run the risk of losing track of who we truly and fully are and little by little come to accept instead the highly edited version which we put forth in hope that the world will find it more acceptable than the real thing."

FREDERICK BUECHNER

PROLOGUE

~~~~~~~~

NOT LONG AFTER we were married, my wife Cathlin and I began reading *Moby-Dick* aloud to each other, a few chapters every evening before we went to bed. We taped each session: although we were young and still imagining our lives, we understood life was fleeting.

When Cathlin's mother died, a few years before our wedding, Cathlin was stunned to realize that the only record of her mother's voice was the outgoing message on the answering machine. And so our idea was that when one of us died, the other would have these tapes and we could be together again, our voices sailing slowly toward some island of solace aboard the *Pequod* with Ishmael and Ahab.

We were living on Martha's Vineyard then, during the off-season. It was 2002, long before children came along, and we were in between things. Cathlin had just finished seminary and I had left the film business. We had come to the island in the solitude of the cold months to polish our résumés and work on our applications—Cathlin to churches and I to graduate schools. We had also come to the island to help my grandmother in her final days.

My ancestors on my mother's side came from a long line of

Vineyarders, stretching back to the early 1700s. The Hardings were whalers, and when the whaling industry faltered, they became shopkeepers on Circuit Avenue in Oak Bluffs. Later, my great-grandfather left the island to look for work and settled in New Jersey, where he raised a family and where I grew up.

My grandparents Bill and Ann Harding met at university in Pennsylvania, set up on a blind date while Ann was attending Moravian and Bill was across the river, at Lehigh. It didn't take long for Bill to introduce his soon-to-be-bride to the Vineyard. Years later, my grandmother described that moment to me: "Your grandfather brought me to this island and there were all these Harding women staring at me, wondering who the heck this skinny girl was, and how she was going to do. Well, I outlived them all. That's how I did."

Gram was proud of her status as the last one standing. But there was a major downside to outliving everyone else of her generation: after she and my grandfather retired, they moved to the island full time to live out their days, and she eventually ended up alone in the old house during the long quiet winters, as the rest of the family lived on the mainland in New Jersey and New York. When we moved out to the Vineyard to be with my grandmother, the doctors didn't know how much time she had—"Maybe a few months, maybe more," they said. So Cathlin and I set up shop a couple of blocks away in a house owned by a friend. We didn't know it would be a test run for returning permanently in a few years.

I spent every summer of my life visiting my grandparents, but I had never lived on the island off-season. I took to it quickly, and so did Cathlin. Our routines were quickly established: I rose early and made the short, cold walk to Gram's house, where I would write for two hours in the old storeroom that had been my bedroom as a child. When Gram woke, we would make coffee and toast and eat breakfast together. After the workday was done—I found a job at a nursery and Cathlin did nonprofit consulting—we all gathered at Gram's for dinner.

During our meals, Cathlin and I would tell Gram about our days, where we traveled on the island, whom we met, what happened at work. If I close my eyes now, I can see the three of us talking. The light outside is gray and there's a slight wind banging against the house. Gram's chair is between Cathlin and me, and she turns from one of us to the other as we talk. I tell her about the four Nepalese guys who were just hired and are suffering terribly from the fall allergies they aren't used to, and about a trucker from off-island who missed the last ferry and was shocked when I told him there were no strip clubs on the island. Gram nods and smiles and tells us stories, too, revealing her life in a way she never had before. She talks about growing up in Pennsylvania, about how poor she and my grandfather were when just starting out, but how happy they were, too. And one night she tells us about the day her eldest daughter died, at the age of twenty-eight.

"I cried so hard and so much that I exhausted all my tears and never cried again," she says.

After washing the dinner dishes, Cathlin and I walk home. We don't have children yet or a television or cell phones, so we take long walks in the evening, listen to the radio, and read. And at the end of the night we turn to *Moby-Dick*, the tape recorder gently whirring beneath our voices.

Gram died that spring, and not long after Cathlin and I packed up our Vineyard lives. The tapes of us reading *Mo-*

by-Dick were put away in an old shoebox and over the years I carried them with me to each new home. When we returned to Martha's Vineyard to raise our two children, I placed the worn box high on the top of a bookcase in our basement. I had never been moved to listen to them—they were a time capsule waiting to be unearthed only in the advent of tragedy.

But eventually I began to wonder what Cathlin and I sounded like back then. And so one dark night not long ago, while my family slept, I pulled the shoebox down from its shelf. If this were a movie, the lid on the box would have creaked and the tapes would have appeared dusty. But nothing was out of the ordinary. I found a tape recorder, inserted a tape, and pressed PLAY.

At first, what I heard was disappointing.

I don't know what I was expecting, but our voices didn't sound very different. I listened as we talked about who would begin reading and where we should place the recorder—the situation felt almost mundane. My voice sounded annoying, too, and I fought the urge to click the tape off immediately and kept listening, alone in the quiet basement.

Finally, Cathlin took over the reading duties, and as Ishmael searched for a ship and was surprised in bed by Queequeg, I remembered the first time I brought Cathlin to the Vineyard. It was a bitterly cold weekend, but on the first day we walked from Oak Bluffs to Edgartown, the wind blowing so hard we had to take shelter behind a small dune. The next day we walked again in the cold from Oak Bluffs to Vineyard Haven, laughed at by the gulls, it seemed, but savoring every moment.

I saw all that again, and then my mind moved forward in time and I saw Cathlin lying in bed, weak from chemotherapy during her breast cancer treatment. I saw our son, Hardy, reading to her from his favorite book and our daughter, Pickle, lying in bed with her mother, buried deep under the covers and slowly caressing her ankles.

And then I was with Gram at her bedside when she could no longer walk. She floated in and out of consciousness. I was sitting beside her, lightly rubbing her face with the tips of my fingers as she once did for me on summer nights when I couldn't sleep, and as my mother does now for my children.

All this I saw and more, so much more, as Ishmael led me out to sea just as my ancestors once led him.

1.

～～

CATHLIN'S CHURCH IS located in the center of Martha's Vineyard, anchoring the town of West Tisbury, about three miles from the parsonage where we live. To say "town" is to imply there *is* one, but along with the church there is only a library, town hall, gas station, post office, take-out restaurant, and general store. Otherwise, West Tisbury is fields and farms with a few roads and streams crisscrossing the land.

The First Congregational Church of West Tisbury is a traditional New England Congregational church: white weathered clapboards with green shutters, a tall steeple with a clock in the tower that is carefully wound by hand each month, and a large bell in the belfry that our daughter rings on Sundays by pulling down on a thick rope. At the very top of the church's spire is a fish-shaped weather vane.

Inside, the church is quiet and bright, with light pouring through the windows. There are pews and Bibles and a large wooden cross behind the pulpit. There is an organ in the balcony, a piano up front. In an adjacent room, there is a kitchen where the church volunteers prepare coffee hour and in the winter cook community suppers for the homeless, the hungry, and the lonely.

Cathlin's church is the sort of small rural church you might see on a postcard. A large rainbow flag hanging over the front door is the only sign that the 350-year-old church isn't mired in a past century. And there is one more clue: on a back wall hangs a hand-painted list of all the pastors going back to when the church was first founded in 1651: *Thomas, John, Experience, Nymphas* . . . and then, in 2008, the first female name: *Cathlin Baker.*

FOR MY FAMILY, the ritual of church doesn't begin with Cathlin in the pulpit, guiding the congregation through the service. The ritual begins in the pews.

A very old islander once told me she had sat in the same pew since she was a little girl: third row, left side. "That's eighty years," she said. "I should have a plaque on the pew but I don't want to stand out." She's a New Englander, proud but not flashy. And very tough. No matter my family's island roots, in these things we are newcomers.

In early 2008, Cathlin applied for the job of solo pastor at the First Congregational Church of West Tisbury. She was forty-one at the time, chief of staff at Union Seminary in New York City and pregnant with our daughter, Eirene, whom everyone has always called Pickle. I was forty-four, a stay-at-home dad to Pickle and then-four-year-old Hardy. There was no way we could afford to live on Martha's Vineyard, but the job came with free housing in the parsonage. Cathlin was offered the pastorship and that summer we moved out to sea, leaving behind New York City, our home for more than twenty years.

In seminary, Cathlin worked as an assistant pastor for a

year, but guiding the First Congregational Church of West Tisbury was her first job leading a church by herself. She had been a hospice chaplain and on staff at Union Seminary, but those were jobs tangential to actually going to church each Sunday. The weekly rhythm of preparing a sermon and bringing the family to the pews was a new one for all of us.

Every Sunday, Cathlin left the house first and I followed, later, with the kids. We quickly became creatures of habit, sitting on the right side, about halfway back from the pulpit. Not too close, not too far away.

A kaleidoscope of the community filled the pews around us. The chief of police usually sat in front of me. Two pews over sat a woman who sold African crafts and put on puppet shows a few times a year. The high school principal and her family sat a few rows behind me, a musician drummed a beat with his fingers on the back of the pew next to me. In summer, famous people stopped by (and still do) and small-town life absorbed the wider world. When Bill Murray visits the church, he doesn't sit in a pew. Instead, he walks upstairs to the choir loft.

The retirees were scattered here and there around the pews—a former writer for *Sports Illustrated*, assorted executives who moved here, and islanders who had always lived here. The head of island hospice. The woman who ran the Alzheimer's care unit at the nursing home. The very tall blind man, whose name I could never remember but who always sat up front—right side, second pew—and each Sunday during prayer time offered up the same three names. After he died, his children, who guided him to his seat, disappeared, too.

Alma Benson sat in front of me. She had worked at Cottle's lumber yard until she was ninety-two years old. If I trace my Martha's Vineyard family tree back far enough, I'm related to the Cottle family. But because we left the island in the mid-1950s, no one seems to know my family history, whereas the Cottles are considered a founding family. After Alma died, her niece Margaret, who always picked her up for church and sat next to her, continued to come every week, and later in the day I would often see her walking alone down one of the winding roads farther up-island.

In our pew, I kept Hardy occupied with coloring books and mazes with John the Baptist at the center of the twists and turns. I'd watch him as he traced a red line with his pen, making a few false starts, backtracking, and then finally giving up in frustration and marking a huge X over John the Baptist's face. Pickle would sit in my lap and arrange her two stuffed animals, a small bear and a bunny, in a conversational circle to chat about how the morning was unfolding.

Hardy and I often played a drawing game. I would put a small squiggle down on the paper, essentially a line with a curve at the end, and hand the paper to Hardy, who would then try to create a picture out of the squiggle. He'd quickly turn it into a tree, then put his own squiggle down for me, and it was my turn to draw. We would go back and forth like this as the church filled up, a community of the faithful on a Sunday morning, with me and the kids looking more like preschool art class.

In those days, with our pew filled with stuffed animals, pencils and paper, Pickle's security blanket, and Lego pieces, parishioners looked at me and smiled as they passed us: the minister's husband at work keeping the kids happy. Not long after Hardy was born, I discovered that a man who publicly takes care of his children is put on a pedestal. A woman who does this is commonplace and noticed only if the kids act up. But for a man, just the attempt to parent publicly is viewed as a success, and a sort of superhero status is granted for no reason at all.

I also got a pass in my role as the minister's husband. No one asked me to bake a pie or chair a committee or host a book group. But I knew that if I were the minister and Cathlin were sitting in the pew, taking care of the kids wouldn't be seen as something special. Not only would she have to bake a lot of pies to measure up, but it would also probably be important for her to be religious. I was given a pass on that, too.

Cathlin, dressed in her black robe and colorful stole, would walk past us down the center aisle toward the front door to greet people as they arrived. She'd smile and Pickle would reach for her, but I held her back, whispering, "Mommy is working." As I did this, I thought about how odd it was that I was essentially spending time at my spouse's office with our kids in tow. What other couple had the same situation? And yet even though I tended to grumble every Sunday, once I was actually in the pew I didn't mind at all.

AFTER THE SERVICE started, Hardy would go to Sunday School. If Pickle felt brave enough, she went, too. Then, for the next forty-five minutes I sat by myself, feeling for a moment like an adult and not just a parent. I would listen to the sermon and let my mind wander without being interrupted by the kids. A church service, with its hymns and prayers, sermon and the passing of the collection plate, seemed old-fashioned and out of sync with the rest of my life, but when I gave in to it, the rest of the world—at least for a moment—vanished.

My favorite part of Cathlin's weekly service was when she asked the congregation to share their joys and concerns, openly or to themselves, and then for several minutes people spontaneously offered up the names of people they were praying for, those who were sick, dying, or struggling. People also spoke to the joy of a sunny day, their children visiting, birthdays, anniversaries, a friend seated with them in the pew. This moment of profound vulnerability never stops being meaningful for me.

After the voices stopped calling out their hopes and joys, their fears and sadness, Cathlin stepped back from the pulpit and sat down. A hush would envelop the church, holding each individual together for some long minutes. These were the moments when I felt like crying, as I sat there and breathed in my life and the lives of those around me.

My true feelings about church and religion are complicated. When my mother stopped making us go to church, I was a teenager and I thought that was the end of it. But then I fell in love with Cathlin, and eventually found myself in a small church on a small island every Sunday, not sure where my life was headed but believing strongly in this holy moment.

The silence was broken with a hymn, and then the lights were dimmed and Cathlin stepped back into the pulpit to deliver her sermon. In those early days I listened mostly as a husband scanning the room and hoping Cathlin was doing well. I also listened as an editor. By the time Cathlin delivered a sermon, I would have read it at least three times and given my feedback.

As part of our weekly routine, every Saturday I wandered the island with the kids in order to give Cathlin the time and space she needed to write. I complained about it, this burden on our every weekend, but when Cathlin texted me from wherever she was writing to say she had a draft and I went home and read her sermon, I was once again struck by the power of our ritual. No matter what else happened during the week, whether we sometimes felt like business managers planning the movements of our children, if we argued or were distant, or if we were too busy to sit and talk, we always had this one shared moment together.

AFTER THE SERMON had been delivered and the hymns sung, I would slip from our pew, collect the children from Sunday School, and, when the weather was warm, walk them to the playground just across the street.

I had spent my boyhood summers living with my grandparents down-island, so this patch of dirt at the island's center was relatively new to me. But from the little park, while pushing Pickle in the baby swing and watching Hardy as he climbed to the top of the slide, I could see almost all of the small town's center, Cathlin's church woven within it.

In the park, we'd wait for Cathlin as the line of parishioners left the church, stopping to shake her hand or hug her before heading to coffee hour or to begin the next part of their day. I didn't quite understand the importance of those interactions on those first Sundays. I hadn't yet seen the baptisms and burials, the weddings and the tragedies that Cathlin would minister to. Nor could I see yet how the community would minister to us in return.

When Cathlin finished her goodbyes, she would join us in the park. She'd sit on the ground with us so her robes blanketed the grass, and the children and I would sit around her.

We had washed ashore, as the island saying goes, not born here but newly arrived from the mainland. But in time, we would come to know what it meant to be islanders.

2.

⁓⁓⁓

T HE FIRST THANKSGIVING after we moved to the Vineyard, a couple in Cathlin's congregation invited us to enjoy
the holiday with them. Twenty years earlier, Paul and Marsha
had traveled the road we were on, moving from New York to
the island to raise their kids. It wasn't an uncommon story.

Paul helped found a public charter school on the island
and was also a cartoonist whose work was often published in
the *New Yorker*. Every Saturday he would create eight gags,
as he called them, and then on Monday take the train to New
York and present them to the cartoon editor. It was a ritual,
he said, and even though the success rate was low and the
commute crazy, he never missed a Saturday-morning drawing session.

Marsha, who volunteered at an island preschool, had
founded an artists collective in Zambia, helping the wom-
en there to find a market for their crafts on the Vineyard
and beyond.

Paul and Marsha's house was small and cozy, and as we
settled in before Thanksgiving dinner, I saw a glimpse of a
life I wanted to create: simple with what appeared to be a
balance of creative pursuits and work to make ends meet.

Paul and I eventually became good friends, forming a bond that included frequent hikes that were more like excuses for long conversations as we walked and reflected on life and living a seasonal existence on this island of two speeds, two incomes, two very different worlds.

But that first Thanksgiving, those hikes were in the future. All I knew that day was what I felt when I held Pickle in my arms and watched Paul and Hardy draw together and Marsha and Cathlin talk on the couch about their work. Thanksgiving has often served as a marker in my life, though not in the traditional sense of simply a day to gather with loved ones to eat turkey. In many ways, it was the ritual of Thanksgiving that brought Cathlin and me together.

CATHLIN AND I met in high school: I was a senior and she was a freshman. We grew up in the same small, working-class town, North Plainfield, New Jersey, at the base of the Watchung Mountains. My family lived on the east end and hers lived on the west end, so we attended different grammar schools and didn't know the other existed until high school.

Our town was in a wealthy county, but the folks in North Plainfield weren't rich. We in North Plainfield were close to the bottom of the list of median incomes, like an anchor dragging down the average. Whereas every other town in our county sat regally at the top of a small mountain range, ours was on the floodplain. When it rained, the water rolled down the hills and into our basements. When the wind blew in from a certain direction, the stink common to sections of the New Jersey Turnpike filled the town. Most parents worked in New Jersey, but a few commuted to New York, like my father, who walked to the train station every weekday morning. Parents in the 1970s were adults who operated mostly off-stage, their comings and goings barely noticed by us kids unless it was dinnertime. Cathlin's parents were an exception. They were older, had lived in New York City for much of their lives, were musicians and beatniks, and seemed cooler and stranger than any of us teenagers could ever hope to be. Her mother, Helen, attended the first US recording session of Ravi Shankar when she worked at Columbia Records. Her father, Alex, at age sixteen ran away from home in Brooklyn when some nuns wanted to perform an exorcism because of his unruly behavior. He joined the Merchant Marine and traveled the world with little more than a set of weights, a Victrola, and a stack of opera records. He was a muscle-bound intellectual who rallied his shipmates with arias and bench presses.

I couldn't help but fall for Cathlin's family first: she was three years younger than I was—a span of time that matters in high school—whereas her brother Alex, my friend, was only a year behind me. This combination, in the complicated dance of youth, meant she was off-limits. But that wasn't really it. When I'm honest with my younger self, I can see that it wasn't the difference in our ages that held me back, and I doubt Alex would have cared if I dated his sister. In truth, I was both attracted to and confused by Cathlin. While the rest of us wandered high school in a muddled haze of fear, boredom, and rampant hormones, Cathlin appeared to have a purpose. A punk rock, skateboard chick, she also played violin in the New Jersey Youth Symphony, and cut school to attend apartheid-divestment rallies in New York City. She wrote for the school newspaper, serious stuff on subjects most of us had never heard of: a series on the Sanctuary Movement, which was a campaign in the 1980s to provide safe haven to Central American refugees; a piece about Harvey Milk High School in New York's East Village; another on gay teen suicide.

In contrast, I viewed schoolwork as a competition, an extension of life on the wrestling mat rather than an intellectual journey. I was so clueless that when Cathlin showed up as wrestling manager, I had no idea it was an attempt to get closer to me, to insert herself into my life, rather than waiting for me to come to her house and hang out with her brother and parents. I thought it was odd that she'd suddenly decided watching two boys in singlets battle it out on a sweat-streaked mat was a fun way to spend her time. So I missed all her signals and dated the other wrestling team manager.

After high school, we stayed in touch. This was long before email, Facebook, or even cellphones. Keeping in touch meant we saw each other once a year at Thanksgiving, when we both returned to the old neighborhood. After college, I settled in New York City and Cathlin moved to Philadelphia.

I can still remember how excited I was during the run-up to each Thanksgiving holiday, knowing we would get together and fill each other in on the trajectories of our lives. We were slowly, layer by layer, adding new memories to our foundation.

We always met up at the Rathskeller, a small dive bar in Dunellen, New Jersey. To enter the Rat, you descended worn, sticky stairs and arrived in a one-room burrow with low ceilings and chipped brick walls. You were greeted by the owner, Fat Larry, whose stomach was so large he couldn't sit facing the bar and instead had to affect a side-saddle mount, parked near the entrance to welcome each patron.

The Rat was always crowded with the faces from high school spanning several years, even generations, and to make the rounds could take all night. But Cathlin and I would edge toward each other and by the end of the evening we'd be sitting next to each other, a pitcher of beer in front of us. Some years she brought a boyfriend with her, and I would eye him suspiciously, an intrusion into the holiday ritual.

At closing time, many of us would go back to Cathlin's parents' house for an after-hours party. The party went on and on, and rather than drive home, I usually stayed and slept on a pull-out couch in the basement. In the morning, after breakfast, I'd hug Cathlin and say, "See you next year."

As the years went on, fewer people turned up at the Rat. One Thanksgiving, when we were in our mid-twenties, none of the usual crowd came home for the holidays, not even Cathlin's brother. It was just Cathlin and me at the bar and later just the two of us back at her parents' house. We stayed up talking, connecting the dots of our lives, very different but also strangely parallel. I had moved to New York City after college for a job in banking but then took myself out of the industry and taught English in Thailand for a year; Cathlin had lived in India, studying the religion of the Dalit people—the "untouchables"—and then moved to Philadelphia to advocate for welfare rights.

But more important, at least at that moment, was that we were both single, although at first this fact didn't hang in the air. We were still just old friends catching up. But then, while setting up the pull-out couch, our shoulders touched. We stopped what we were doing and looked at each other. We were about to kiss when there was a loud thump upstairs.

"It's probably my parents," Cathlin said. "I'll tell them we're home."

As I watched her walk up the stairs, I thought the moment to kiss her had been lost. I was surprised by the speed of her return, but she was shaking her head and looked frightened.

"Something's not right up there," she said. "I'm afraid to go into the kitchen."

We silently went upstairs, with me in the lead. All was quiet until I gently opened the door to the kitchen. Then there was a rush of movement: a flash of jeans and a dark jacket racing across the room, shoving aside the kitchen table and knocking over a chair. A man darted for the open window, leaped out, and disappeared into the night.

The house erupted in activity. Cathlin's parents rushed from their bedroom, followed by her sister and brother-in-law. They came clattering down the stairs and then we all stood, motionless for a second, in the kitchen.

"A burglar—on Thanksgiving night!" Cathlin's mother said. The man had stolen her purse, which had been on a table near the window, and hidden behind the door when he first heard Cathlin's footsteps as she walked up from the basement.

We called the police. Two officers arrived, one of whom was a kid we had known in high school. Now he had a mustache and a badge. The cop grilled Cathlin and me about the break-in. He wanted to know every detail, including what we were doing in the basement. I wanted to shout, "About to fulfill my lifelong dream!" Instead, I said, "Nothing," which seemed to seal my fate. Rather than asking Cathlin for a date—after all, I now knew she was interested in me—I retreated under the weight of nerves.

A decade of watching from afar is not easily overcome.

Too timid to do anything else, I tried a side route and called a friend in Philadelphia, where Cathlin was living.

"Tom," I said, "I have to start visiting you . . . a lot."

"What?" he said. "Why?"

"Well, there's this girl, and I'm in love with her."

I took the train to Philadelphia four times in the next two months. Each trip turned out to be more excruciating than the last. I would call Cathlin, casually mentioning I was in town, and she'd go out with us. But now that I had a real purpose, had stated my desire to myself and to my friend, I lost the ability to be myself around her, to just relax and talk to her.

This new approach was so awkward and painful that I gave up—not just on going to Philadelphia, but also on Cathlin. I even stopped calling her when I was back in New Jersey for the occasional holiday.

Years passed and we lost touch—I didn't even know where she lived.

Then, one evening just before Labor Day, I got call from Pete, a mutual friend from high school. He had tragic news: his parents had died in a horrific accident. While they were visiting Colorado, a truck ran a red light and crashed into their car, killing both of them instantly. At the end of the call, Pete said he couldn't bear telling the story over and over and asked if I could tell Cathlin's family what had happened and about the service, which would be held in our hometown.

I called Cathlin's brother, and during the course of the conversation, Alex suggested I contact Cathlin—maybe we could ride home together.

"What?" I asked.

"Don't you know she lives in New York City now?" he said.

Cathlin had moved to the city just weeks earlier to attend

Union Theological Seminary, on the Upper West Side. I had
been living in the city for almost a decade by then, and not
only had I never been to the seminary, I'd never even heard
of it. But there I was, a few days later, parked in front of the
massive Gothic building and eyeing it suspiciously as I waited for Cathlin.

During the drive to New Jersey, Cathlin and I didn't talk
much. It wasn't because of a wall of uncertainty and anxiety
I had constructed—now there was something real in the air.
A friend's parents, two people who had meant a great deal
to me as a boy, were dead. Small talk was impossible, and I
didn't know how to talk about pain and sadness. Quiet felt
right, the two of us going home together.

At the funeral, I didn't know what to say to Pete and his
brothers and resorted to shrugs, hugs, and avoidance. But
Cathlin didn't hide. I watched as she comforted Pete and his
brothers, marveling anew at her poise. She appeared to hold
not only Pete in her arms but his grief, too, and even the
weight of the two closed coffins resting side by side at the
church's altar.

Back at the wake, I approached Cathlin. I was on my
way to attend my older brother's wedding, which, coin-
cidentally, was about to take place a few blocks away. I
stepped close to her and took one of her hands. Her mother
later told me she witnessed this moment and it had given
her goosebumps. For me, it was more of a jolt, as though
an electrical current finally switched on, set free to flow
through my body.

"When we get back to New York, let's go out," I said. "On
a date."

"I'd like that," Cathlin said. "I'd like that very much."

I ONCE ATTENDED a reading by the Pulitzer Prize–winning nonfiction writer Tracy Kidder. He told a story about when he was beginning the book *Mountains Beyond Mountains*—the story of Paul Farmer, a brilliant doctor and health advocate for the poor who set up clinics in rural Haiti. His editor brought up the "problem" of goodness in the narrative. The editor worried that as a protagonist, Farmer was all good, which might come across as unreal or, even worse, uninteresting.

Kidder said he looked for the dark side of Farmer but all he could find was a man whose biggest "fault" might be that he was driven too hard to save the world's poor. The problem of goodness stayed in Kidder's mind; his solution was to insert himself into the narrative more overtly than he'd done in previous books. He needed a baseline, he said, not the opposite of "goodness," but rather normalcy—that is, a man not brilliant or driven to do good, but instead one who was surprised at every step of the journey. Kidder became that foil.

I often feel this way about myself in relation to Cathlin.

Cathlin is *good* but not in the sense of *pious*. She drinks and swears and can become undone in the daily struggle of life, but she's *good* to the core in a way I can't ever see myself.

Eight years after our first date, Cathlin and I married.

3.

A FEW MONTHS AFTER our move to the island, Hardy
began acting out. He wasn't sleeping well, and his temper flared at the slightest provocation: socks were a frequent
adversary; he didn't want to get in the car and he didn't want
to get out of the car; play dates were no fun for anyone. In
general, he was a pain in the ass.

Once a month a child psychologist visited the island, to
check in with the various agencies and her clients. The service was free, a nod from the state not to forget about those
few souls living out on the ocean; in the winter, the Vineyard
has one of the highest rates of unemployment and alcohol-
ism in the state.

We met with the woman, and she agreed to observe Hardy
at preschool. A few weeks later we sat down with her again.

"He's grieving," she said. "He's grieving the loss of his
home in New York City. He's moving through the stages of
grief and at the moment is stuck on anger."

This made a lot of sense, as I had come to realize that I
was grieving too. I was a stay-at-home dad when we lived
in New York City, which gnawed at my pride, but at least in
the city there was company in the trenches. The playgrounds

and parks were crowded with moms and nannies for me to chat with. I could sit with Hardy in his stroller at a café and pretend I was part of the greater world, that I was happy.

But the Vineyard was lonely and dreary in the off-season. In summer the population swells to more than 100,000, but come September the summer people begin to leave. And every week more and more people leave, so that by January the population has shrunk to about 5,000. Stores close, too, until it's mostly just the gas stations, grocery stores, and a few restaurants with their lights still on.

It took me months to find a mom-friend on the island, and I had no idea what work I would do here. I had taken a leap of faith, following Cathlin to the place of my ancestors but now felt disconnected from my past and present. I grieved for my former life and for my future one, too. The only through-line in my life was a desire to write.

While working in banking and then the film industry, I scribbled on the side, taking classes at night and getting up early in the morning to write before heading off to work. But I had nothing to show for it, never put out into the world what I had scribbled. And what I'd written wasn't very good, anyway. That's not modesty: I hadn't found what I needed to write about. And so, on the Vineyard, I turned to what was in front of me—my family.

I recall taking an after-dinner stroll with our children. Hardy crashed ahead in the woods; Pickle walked closer to me but not with me, slowly becoming a small creature of the wider world rather than just something in my orbit. She walked without looking back to see if I was following. I felt a tug at my heart. My daughter has always been a bit of a mystery to me. The same is true of my son, but I do know more about the workings of a young boy, having been one myself.

I watched Pickle, a mere ten paces in front of me, but already I knew that in the blink of an eye she would travel so much farther away.

I looked out at the woods. The sun hovered just above the tree line, spreading dappled light among the leaves, burnt orange and red. I breathed deeply, then turned back to watch my daughter again.

She stopped walking and looked at me.

"Dada," she said, "will you keep me safe?

There are times when life feels as if it's hurtling along, a high-speed motor attached to every moment until days rush by in a blur. Everything becomes gray with motion when we go about the business of living. And then there are other moments so heavy with meaning that the earth seems to pause on its axis. This moment in the woods with my children was one of those.

There was no immediate worry. No approaching car nor overeager dog. And yet Pickle felt the need to check in, using words so loaded that my knees buckled. I ran the ten paces to her, scooped her up in my arms, and kissed her soft cheek.

"Yes, yes," I said. "I'll always keep you safe."

Pickle smiled, asked to be let down, then ran ahead again. In a few steps she tripped on a root, falling to the ground and scraping her knee.

I carried Pickle into the house and took care of her cut. I wiped it clean, applied some ice and then ointment, and made the small drops of blood disappear behind a Hello Kitty adhesive.

Hardy joined us inside. At first he seemed insensitive to Pickle's injury, going on about a squirrel he had seen in the woods while Pickle sniffled on the couch. Then he became annoying, asking me repeatedly for a cup of water.

"Can't you see I'm busy?" I finally shouted, losing my temper.

He began to cry, but I ignored him while I continued to help Pickle, drying the tears from her eyes and wrapping her in a cozy blanket. Then I looked over at my son, sitting alone on the stairs, weeping softly to himself.

Pickle's words echoed in my head: "Dada, will you keep me safe?"

I looked at her sitting contentedly on the couch. How quickly I had failed to keep her safe from even the most trivial of accidents, a root in her path. Then I looked at my son. Was I keeping him safe, letting him cry alone on the stairs?

I stood and went to Hardy, lifted him off the stairs, and brought him over to the couch. Then I sat between my children and with an arm around each, I hugged them tightly, determined to keep them both safe, if only for one fleeting and fragile moment.

4.

~~~

A S A BOY, staying with my grandparents during summers on the Vineyard, one of my jobs to earn a weekly allowance was to walk up street to the post office in Oak
Bluffs and pick up the mail.

The post office was filled with old mailboxes with small
combination locks you twisted once to the right, once to the
left, and then back to the right again. Our box was knee-high
for an adult but almost eye level for me. I felt like a spy, turning the combination until I heard it click, then opening the
small door to retrieve the letters and bills. Two days a week,
on Tuesday and Friday, the letters and bills were tucked inside a folded copy of the *Vineyard Gazette*.

Back home, I distributed the mail and then took the
newspaper to the porch and spread it out on the floor. It was
a broadsheet, far too large for me to hold open with my short
arms. I read the movie listings and looked for a poem by my
grandfather. I checked the tide chart for the right time to
fish and read the profiles of islanders I wanted to be like,
tough men and women who worked the water, as my ancestors did, instead of running away from the island to live in
New Jersey.

The *Vineyard Gazette* was founded in 1846, and since that time has recorded just about everything about island life. Not long after we moved to the Vineyard, I began submitting essays to the paper via the general email address. I never heard anything, but a few weeks later the *Gazette* would publish my most recent essay. There were no emails back and forth about edits, nor was there any payment. I was a ghost, the editors were ghosts, but my words were real because they appeared in print.

I continued to send essays to the paper, and eventually I noticed a short bio at the bottom of one of my pieces. Set in italic, it read: *Bill Eville lives in West Tisbury.* At some point, it was switched to: *Gazette contributor Bill Eville lives in West Tisbury.*

5.

~~~

When Cathlin was an assistant minister at Judson Memorial Church, in New York City, her office was located at the bottom of Washington Square Park in Lower Manhattan. At the time, we lived in Washington Heights, way farther north. One day, Cathlin asked me to help clean her office and carry a few boxes of books back to our small apartment.

While I packed the books, I buried the most glaringly religious titles—like the Bible—on the bottom. Such was my state of mind then that openly hauling around a box full of porn would have caused me less discomfort than if someone saw me with a set of religious books.

On the long subway ride home, I grew bored and began picking through one of the boxes. I chose *Telling Secrets*, by the theologian Frederick Buechner. It was the third book in his series of memoirs and in the prologue he wrote: "It is important to tell at least from time to time the secret of who we truly and fully are—even if we tell it only to ourselves—because otherwise we run the risk of losing track of who we truly and fully are and little by little come to accept instead the highly edited version which we put forth in hope that the world will find it more acceptable than the real thing."

I was thinking about Buechner's words when some drunken young men got on at a Midtown stop. They were loud and boisterous. One sat next to me, another stood hanging on to the pole, one arm draped casually around it. The other two sat on the opposite side and took turns slugging each other in the arm.

As we rattled along, the drunk next to me peered over my shoulder, and soon asked what I was reading.

"It's my wife's," I said, trying to point the finger of blame elsewhere. With my heel, I nudged the boxes further under the seat.

The drunk nodded. "What's it about?" he asked. He smiled. He wasn't a belligerent drunk—he seemed sort of goofy, but as though he really wanted to know what the book was about.

Something about his smile, combined with the passage I had just read, about telling our secrets, made me answer truthfully. I looked into his glazed eyes and said something I'd been having difficulty saying to even my closest friends.

"My wife is a minister."

There it was, on the table. I'd said it simply and out loud . . . albeit to a drunken stranger. But it was a start. At that time, my wife's vocation was so foreign and unsettling to me that I couldn't speak *of* it; I had to speak *around* it and then drown the listener in qualifications. "She's not a fanatic," I'd explain. "She doesn't go door to door trying to convert anyone." Heck, "She's not even into God," I once heard myself saying. "It's more of a social justice thing."

The drunk looked at me. His smile faded from one of curiosity to one of puzzlement, and a deep crease appeared on his brow. Then he smiled again.

"All right!" he said, turning toward his buddies. "This guy's banging a minister!" He held up his open palm to me for a high five.

"Well, that's one way to put it," I said, and returned his high five.

IT MAY SEEM odd for a minister's husband to admit to not being religious, and that I was once afraid to tell even my closest friends that my girlfriend went to seminary. And it was strange, compartmentalizing my love for Cathlin, separating her from her life at seminary and in the church. But as a teenager, I'd given up going to church after my mother—the force driving us there every Sunday—lost her faith. Plus, I could rely on my love for Cathlin before church was part of her life. Because I had heard about and not experienced firsthand the steps in between—she majored in religion in college, studied the subject in India, and later decided to enter seminary—I was able to ignore what was in front of me. When we first started dating and I picked her up at Union Theological Seminary, I tended to keep my head down to avoid anything I feared might be theologically contagious.

It also helped that Cathlin told me she was not going to seminary in order to lead a church. For her, it was an extension of her social justice work, and she even graduated without the credentials to become a minister. But a few years later, after her mother died, Cathlin felt what ministers refer to as their "call experience." She was in a small hotel room in Cuba, at an international women's rights conference, still grieving the loss of her mother. As she told it to me later,

31

her room went from black and white to Technicolor and she heard the words: *Anything is possible.*

When Cathlin returned home, she said she needed to go back to Union, this time in a master of divinity program, the path to becoming a minister. By that time, I had softened a little and become more accustomed to her world. This was due in no small part to her classmates, now friends of mine and people I admired. They were all down-to-earth and funny, but something larger, too. They seemed to move more comfortably in the world by acknowledging and fighting back against how uncomfortable the world was for so many. They didn't appear to live in the past or abide by some dusty book of rules. Instead, they viewed the Bible as a living thing to be interpreted and argued with, to lay a foundation that began and ended with inclusivity and goodness.

But most of all, they seemed like regular people—like Cathlin—so I could continue to pretend their faith had nothing to do with why I liked them so much. But then, like so many stories in the Bible, I was sent into the valley of darkness. Eventually, I was led out by a group of rabble-rousing nuns.

WHEN CATHLIN WORKED at Judson Church, I worked in the film business as a development executive looking for material and helping writers adapt a book or play or magazine article into a screenplay. My office was located just a few blocks from Cathlin's church, and we often met in the middle for lunch. I liked the work, but I also took writing classes at night at a place called the Writer's Studio and had begun to imagine a life for myself that involved my own writing and not just helping others succeed on the page. But that was too big a leap of faith for me, so when a business opportunity arose that seemed a perfect hybrid, I went for it. The idea was to create a hive of writers, on salary, all working on material together. I would help run the company but also be one of those writers.

The business venture failed quickly and spectacularly when the man fronting the money turned out to have none. Dark days followed, the type of darkness that, once a bit of normalcy and light has been restored, can only be remembered with a shake of the head and the words, "Man, those were *dark days . . .*"

But when you're adrift in the darkness, you're not even aware that you've been swallowed up. Mind-numbing despair and confusion became my reality. I was unable to get off the couch because I no longer understood who I was, without an office to go to or coworkers to laugh and complain with. My sense of direction felt so broken, my self-worth so low, that I couldn't even conceive of looking for another film job.

I did understand that I had attempted the ill-fated venture because I wanted to escape the seventy-hour work weeks of the movie business and try for what I loved: writing. But after the venture failed, I spent my time cursing myself for even attempting to change my life.

Finally, after months of wallowing in a funk, I rose from the couch, but only out of necessity: I needed to find work. The job I found was in a building—referred to as the "God Box"—in Upper Manhattan, on Riverside Drive. It did look like a box, a lump set down on a corner with no architectural flair, no curves or spires, no distinguishing characteristics at all, which of course made it stand out. The God Box was home to the offices of a number of religious communities, a sort of headquarters for the managerial structures of spirituality. Here, the accountants and long-range planners, the church pension fund managers and health care specialists gathered and toiled. And it was into the God Box I walked one day after Cathlin helped me off the couch as she said, "You have to do something."

She had found me a temporary job assisting to organize a conference on the environment and spirituality. I would be the database guy, both inputting the information of registrants and handling outreach. I had gone from working in film, a job that was at least glamorous at times, with screening rooms and expense-account lunches and dinners, to answering the phone and plugging numbers into spreadsheets. I loved it.

When the conference ended and a woman I had met in the cafeteria offered me a job helping to run her office, I said yes, even though I didn't actually know what her office did.

Sister Eileen was the first to greet me. She smelled of cigarettes, which she later told me she smoked in her car, not so much to be out of view but because she liked to smoke with the windows up—a full immersion for her limit of two cigarettes a day.

Sister Eileen, like Sister Carol and Sister Carmen, was a liaison for her order to the United Nations. The three nuns traveled about, it seemed to me, incognito: they didn't wear habits or cluster in a convent, living instead in small apartments like regular folk. And they were funny. Until that point, my interactions with nuns were zero. To my generation, they appeared on television and the movies as either pious and wise or mean and unyielding. Their personas, I had thought, fit my narrow view of organized religion, that it was stuck in time and offered little to nothing of value to the modern-day enlightened.

But my new officemates in the God Box were a group of devout women who were also incredibly politically savvy and so tough that they thought Mother Teresa was a bit of an enabler because she fetishized poverty rather than railing against the socioeconomic and political root causes of it. These were women who were spiritual, had dedicated their lives to God, and yet none of them were about to blindly follow any guidelines mere humans had laid out for them. In their tradition they were both lauded and treated as second-class citizens. Nuns couldn't be ordained, and until Vatican II didn't enjoy much freedom at all. But they had remained steadfast and carved out a niche because they believed a life dedicated to God was the only one worth living.

So, there I was, going to work each day with a bunch of nuns, and at the end of the day coming home to a minister. And yet I still felt uncomfortable about the whole idea of organized religion.

I began to hang out with my nun friends more and more. Eventually, our long lunches turned into spending time at their homes. I convinced Sister Eileen and Sister Carol to sit down with me for interviews during which I would run my tape recorder and ask them about their lives, what they were like as kids and when they experienced a calling to enter their orders. I asked them about the challenges they faced, and both said their parents were against their becoming nuns.

In an attempt to expand my thinking about religion, I went on a three-day retreat of silence and fasting at Genesis Farm, in Blairstown, New Jersey. Sister Miriam, who ran the retreat, lived in a straw-bale house on the property and for three days I and seven other seekers were her students. By day I sat in the woods and at night I sat on a small cot in my room, retching until morning, not because I was physically hungry—I knew about dry heaves from dieting as a wrester—but because of a deeper hunger, an emotional upheaval I was just beginning to understand.

Later, back at the office, I spoke about this one afternoon with Sister Sonia, a Brazilian nun with the Missionary Sisters of the Holy Spirit. Sister Sonia was small and thin. She wore large glasses and tweed sport coats and said things like, "Today I have the anger of lion!" while taking a swipe at the air with her fingers bent like claws.

"It's strange," I said to her. "I'm married to a minister and work with nuns, but I'm not a religious man." We were eating lunch and I spoke between bites of my sandwich.

Sister Sonia looked at me. "And what makes you think you are not religious?" she asked.

I talked for a while about my thoughts about the whole idea of religion, and my belief that God and all that crazy stuff in the Bible seemed more suited for a time when people still thought the world was flat. Sister Sonia nodded quietly and after a bit she smiled and touched my arm.

"Bill," she said, "I say no a lot. I say no too much in my life. For a long time I even said no to learning English because of my anger with what the United States had done to my country. But after a while, I realized that saying no was making my life small—so I forced myself to say yes. And I continued to say yes to everything for a whole year. I called it My Year of Grace.

"Saying yes has not been easy," she continued. "I left my home because I said yes. I had to learn a new language. I have to ride the subway." She made a face and raked the air with her fingers. "But it has brought me here to this moment and this conversation. Saying yes has enabled us to meet. Saying yes is an act of faith."

Going home on the bus that afternoon, I thought about what Sister Sonia had said, and what Frederick Buechner had written about our needing to stop from time to time to tell ourselves who we really are as opposed to the edited version we create for others. And then right there on the M4 bus, I began to feel a small crack in my wall of no.

The failure of my business venture had left me so distraught that I'd forgotten why I chose to try it in the first place: because my work in the film industry, helping other writers achieve success, was an endless exercise in keeping my own self hidden. My refusal to at least be curious about the presence of God was another example of this. I was holding on to opinions formed when I was a child, when turning my back on anything mysterious made me feel in control of my life. The impossibility of being in control had never occurred to me, just like it hadn't occurred to me that by saying no to the mystery of God, I might also be saying no to the mystery of my own self.

So I began to say yes.

I didn't go hog-wild and say yes to everything, as Sister Sonia had done, but proceeded slowly, beginning with the realization that I was searching for something. And as I gradually let go, a strange thing occurred: I saw that my yes wasn't yes to a belief or even to a way of life. In fact, it wasn't even yes to the dictionary meaning.

As Sister Sonia told me, saying yes is an act of faith, not a negotiation that allows you to make up spiritual terms, such as, "Hey, if I do this, this, and this, then I get that, that, and that." Saying yes is frightening. Sometimes it can feel more like losing your life than finding it, more like darkness than light, more like realizing how incredibly tiny and insignificant you really are.

A FEW MONTHS after my talk with Sister Sonia, she announced she was being transferred to Rome. Cathlin and I helped her pack and one snowy day in January drove her to the airport, where we hugged and promised to stay in touch and see each other again.

Years later, Cathlin and I did go to Rome, for our honeymoon. We stayed with Sister Sonia just outside the city in her convent, along with about fifty other members of the Missionary Sisters of the Holy Spirit. And soon after we returned home, I went back to school, at the age of thirty-eight, to get a master's degree in creative writing.

6.

⁓⁓⁓

TWO YEARS AFTER we'd settled on the island, I read in the *Vineyard Gazette* a job listing for the paper itself, a low-level calendar editor, and I sent in an inquiry. To my surprise, I was asked to come in immediately for an interview.

"We pay terribly," the editor, Julia Wells, told me. She was right; it was barely more than minimum wage.

In hindsight, I realize the paper was desperate for a body to fill a chair. That I had no experience in journalism didn't matter. I worked with words and had a long history with the island—that was enough, as the busy summer season was about to begin.

"I'll take it," I told Julia, just as desperate as she was. I needed to get out of the house again after so many years as a stay-at-home dad, to be in the company of adults. I had begun to worry that my life, which had always consisted of starting over again as I moved not just from job to job but also from industry to industry, had reached a dead end, and that I was quickly growing too old for another do-over.

Near the end of my first day at the paper, Cathlin called to ask me how it was going. I was almost in tears. I had spent the day doing data entry, typing in the listings for the paper's

39

calendar, four pages of events taking place over the course of the following week. It was late June and the events kept coming and coming, from library story times to photography workshops and art openings. "This is my new life," I whined to Cathlin, "a Bartleby existence, chained to my desk while the world outside churns ahead." I almost left that first day; but I had nowhere to go.

The next day our Tuesday edition went to press and the pace slackened. We could catch our breath and prepare for Friday's edition. There were no listings to input. I realized Father's Day was the next weekend and asked Julia if I could write an essay. When she said yes, I returned to my desk and for the first time in my life spent the next few hours writing at work as part of my job. I didn't have to hide the fact that I was writing or sneak outside to write a few more sentences, as I'd done at so many jobs. My job was to write—it was what my paycheck asked of me.

7.

MY FATHER LOVED to mow the lawn. In fact, he enjoyed all manner of chores—the mending, taming, and building that a house and yard require were always his domain. As a young boy, I used to watch him, ducking behind bushes or trees whenever he stopped to rest and looked around.

During the summer, my father would take me to play golf. We would rise, the two of us, at dawn, and were always the first at the course; only the morning dew preceded us. Both of our sets of clubs were in one bag, my father carrying it while I used a five iron to make my way up the fairway, the front of my sneakers soggy, speckled with sticky blades of newly mown grass. I can see my father's head bent in concentration over his ball and hear his voice as it rises above the treetops. "Attaboy!" he'd call out whenever I hit a clean shot.

In the evenings we played tennis. There were always morning games, too, but those were for the family, whereas the evening games were reserved for the two of us. Our volleys lasted a long time, the ball coming in fast but somehow always within reach. I didn't question this rather astounding fact, but now I understand that my father was keeping me in the game. I can feel the sweat drying on my body as the sun dropped behind the trees, now a bit chilly, and my father and I driving home in the dark, very late for dinner but not hungry at all.

Now, so many years later, I was the one mowing the lawn, stopping for a moment to wipe the sweat from my forehead and noticing Hardy dressed in a flowing green cape, pirate tricorn, and a pair of flippers. He was lurking near the shed, watching me. I pretended not to see him and started the mower again.

Hardy would also watch me write. He was always an early riser and on some mornings would join my dawn writing sessions by coming into the basement room where I worked. I was never worried I'd lose my train of thought. We had a routine, the two of us: he waved to me and I waved back, then he got out his Legos and on the floor began to build.

Occasionally I watched him. And when, from time to time, he'd look over at me, I would duck and turn away, thinking of those days when I loved to watch my father, when he was young and strong, like a planet I joyfully floated around.

8.

ONE WET AND chilly morning, I suggested to Pickle that she put on a coat before going outside. Giving my children suggestions about what clothes to wear was a battle I waged almost daily for years, neither side willing to concede defeat. The fact that at age eight I drove my parents mad by wearing the same green T-shirt every day for an entire summer didn't stop me from attempting to get them clothed appropriately.

Pickle glared at me and shook her head. She was wearing purple shorts, an Ozzy Osborne T-shirt (amazing what you find in a hand-me-down box), and her mother's high-heeled shoes. She looked like an aging carny.

"How about I kick you back to Buffalo," she snarled.

Pickle's retort—as if we were two men at the pub disagreeing and about to take it outside—caught me off guard. Then I realized she was riffing on a lyric from the new man in her life and I felt a rush of fatherly pride. The man's name was Mr. Bruce Springsteen.

I grew up in New Jersey, where the Boss was essential to life, like breathing and playing baseball. He made going to the Jersey Shore a mythic journey, one that could bring out our hopes and dreams and make them seem attainable. But I hadn't been pushing the Boss on my daughter. Honest. He came into Pickle's life in the most unlikely manner.

Cathlin returned one evening from a leadership conference at which the facilitator had used Springsteen's conducting in the *Seeger Sessions*, an album of traditional music, as an example of excellent leadership. The family gathered on the couch to check out the DVD and watch Springsteen work with his band on the intro to "Fifteen Miles on the Erie Canal."

The next morning, while driving with the radio on, Pickle yelled from the backseat, "Turn this off, I want Bruce Springsteen!"

We were soon in the land of obsession.

Pickle refused to listen to anyone else, especially women. "No girls," she demanded whenever I turned the stereo on. Even the young Boss wouldn't do. No *Born to Run* or *Darkness on the Edge of Town*. *Nebraska* fared okay for a bit until Cathlin caught the two of us on the couch listening to "Johnny 99."

"That's about a man on death row," she reminded me.

But it wasn't only when we listened to music that Bruce dictated our lives.

One night in the bathroom, when Pickle was in the early stages of her toilet training and still comfortable with it being a communal affair, she asked me to leave the room. I nodded and sat out in the hallway, my back to the wall. Soon she began to sing a song from the *Seeger Sessions*: "Oh, Mary, don't you weep, don't you mourn / Oh, Mary, don't you weep, don't you mourn / Didn't Pharaoh's army get drowned? / Oh, Mary, don't you weep."

When you become a parent, you know your life will change and that you'll experience something new. But nothing can prepare you for these moments: a sudden respite from the multiple agendas of life to a quiet interlude seated outside the bathroom listening to your three-year-old daughter singing gospel songs while trying to go potty.

Sitting in the hallway, I was sent back to another evening of waiting. Almost three decades earlier, my buddy Dave Serido and I spent a night in lawn chairs outside a strip mall in central New Jersey waiting to buy Springsteen tickets in the morning. There were hundreds of other fans spending the night, too. Some people had coolers, others were grilling, and during the night our friends, Snakehead, Boog, Guzzi, and Paulie C.—all of them scattered now and navigating their own midlife terrains—stopped by to check on us and supply us with more beer. I had just finished my freshman year in college. When I think of that time now, it feels like a life lived by someone else, sprawled in a lawn chair with my high school friends, all of us spirits in the night and excited to be sleeping in a parking lot.

OTHER THAN MYSELF and an imaginary father Pickle called Bob Cheeks, the Boss was my daughter's first crush. I was heartened by her choice. A genuine star with deep moral values. But sitting outside the bathroom door, thinking of my teens, I also knew it would not be Pickle's last love affair.

I could only hope that if, as a teenager, she brought home some leather-clad suitor and I stared aghast as he blustered about it being their "one last chance to make it real," I'd remember that moment outside the bathroom and find some kind of solace in the knowledge that even as a mere preschooler, my daughter could take the measure of a good man.

9.

A HIGHLIGHT OF AUGUST is the Martha's Vineyard Agricultural Society Livestock Show & Fair, known as simply the Ag Fair. Founded in 1858, the fair stretches across four days and includes carnival rides and games of chance, and woodsmen contests with various formidable acts of wood chopping while tree climbing. Every summer, we took the kids for the racing pigs and acrobats, corn dogs and funnel cake, and each year I was struck by how unchanged the fair remained, decade after decade.

I remember one summer when Cathlin and the kids wandered off as soon as we entered the fairgrounds, and I found myself standing alone, watching children twirl in the sun, teenagers exchanging high-fives, and locals reconnecting after a busy summer working three jobs. Then I noticed another man staring out at the same view. He was wearing blue overalls and a baggy shirt, looking very much like a local farmer. But when he turned, I saw it was John Mellencamp.

It's common courtesy to ignore the celebrities who summer here, to give them their space so they can be regular folk for a while. And at first I did sort of ignore Mellencamp— who I knew in my youth as John Cougar—while I also watched him out of the corner of my eye. His girlfriend, Meg Ryan, was in a long line for food and the line wasn't moving, and so I decided to approach Mellencamp.

"I bet no one has ever told you this," I said, "but you helped me win a lot of wrestling matches."

Mellencamp looked at me, sort of wide-eyed, as if I had woken him from a trance.

"How so?" he asked.

"Your music," I told him. "It helped psych me up before matches, back in high school."

Mellencamp stood still for a beat, then bent his knees and got in a stance, his hands up and ready.

"Wanna wrestle?" he asked.

I assumed a wrestling stance, too, and for a moment it looked as if another fair attraction was about to begin. Instead, we smiled and settled for a fist bump.

I WENT LOOKING for Cathlin and the kids and found them waiting in line for the Rotor, a centrifugal ride that made me sick even as a young kid. They handed the man their tickets and I stepped back and watched them disappear inside the ride. And as I watched the ride gather force and begin spinning, I was sent back in time, exiting the same ride with my older brother, Jim, holding my stomach and groaning, "No more."

I was eleven years old, Jim two years older, and we were finally old enough to go to the fair by ourselves. We lived down-island in Oak Bluffs and it was a long ride to the fair. When my mother dropped us off, she gave explicit instructions that if we couldn't find a lift home from someone we knew, we were to use a pay phone and call home for a ride.

This was the summer of 1977 and then, as now, Martha's Vineyard was a friend to hitchhikers. Riding around with my grandfather, we often picked up hitchhikers, singles or groups of older kids, even adults sometimes. As a kid I spent a lot of time on the porch reading and inserting myself into the thrilling new worlds I found in books, and hitchhikers seemed to me the very embodiment of adventure. When we picked up a hitchhiker, I moved to the backseat so the person could sit next to my grandfather, who liked to ask each new potential friend about his life and what he enjoyed most about the island.

At the end of our first parentless night at the Ag Fair, when the summer sky had turned dark and Jim and I had our fill of dart throwing, the tilt-a-whirl, and snow cones, we decided hitchhiking would be a much more grown-up and exciting way to get home.

Neither of us had hitchhiked before but it seemed easy enough. We stood at the exit of the fairgrounds and put our thumbs up. We were two young boys standing before a stream of cars forced to stop at the exit before turning onto the street. Almost instantly a man driving alone motioned for us to get in his car. He was headed to Edgartown, not Oak Bluffs, but we were eager for the adventure, so we climbed in anyway. He seemed friendly and I assumed that when we reached Edgartown he would take us the rest of the way home. But he stuck to his plan and dropped us just outside Edgartown, more than six miles from our grandparents' cottage in Oak Bluffs.

Jim and I stood at the side of the road with our thumbs up, but what few cars we saw continued on without slowing down. After about thirty minutes we decided to jog along Beach Road, which cuts through two bodies of water, Sengekontacket Pond on one side, Vineyard Sound on the other. Out there in the dark we could hear the waves hitting the beach; the only other sound was our breathing, which became more labored as we ran. We made it almost to the Big Bridge before a mix of exhaustion and too many snow cones slowed us to a walk.

It's been several decades since that night and yet I can still see quite clearly my brother and me standing on the road at the edge of the beach. I wasn't frightened because I was with my big brother. Jim always knew what to do—or at least appeared to know—so I never felt afraid of anything. It's the path of so many younger siblings to act out in order to get attention from their parents. But I never saw any reason for this: the one whose attention I wanted most of all was my brother, and for this I never lacked.

The road near Big Bridge was quiet and what few cars came along drove past, their headlights illuminating us for a moment before disappearing in the dark. Jim and I discussed jogging again, but instead sat down where the sand met the road, leaning against each other, back to back, so we could watch the road from both directions. We would take a ride back to Edgartown even, where at least we could call home for a ride. It was only ten o'clock, but it felt much later.

I was tired but happy. In a few weeks we would go home to New Jersey. I would enter the seventh grade, and Jim would start his first year of high school. His new beginning felt like an end to me. Going to high school didn't mean leaving me, not in the literal sense, but it felt momentous. Jim had muscles now, hair on his upper lip, and all the usual physical signs that he was changing. But out there on the beach that night, he was still all mine.

"I see headlights," Jim said.

I turned around and saw yellow lights cutting away at the distant darkness. We stood, lifted our arms, and put our thumbs up. With my free hand, I shielded my eyes from the bright headlights as they came closer and felt the rush of wind push me back as the car raced by. A wave of disappointment filled me. But then, almost immediately, I heard the screech of tires. I turned and saw the back of the car shudder and fishtail before coming to a stop about thirty yards away.

I ran to the car, opened the back door, and slid across the seat to make room for Jim. My brother had barely closed the door behind him when the driver hit the accelerator and we skidded back onto the road.

There were three people up front. The driver sat hunched over the wheel smoking a cigarette. A woman sat next to him and beside her sat a very tall man, his head almost touching the roof of the car, his hair hanging past his shoulders. It didn't take long to realize that this wasn't going to be a ride like the ones in our grandfather's car.

Nobody turned around to welcome us or ask us about our lives, not even when I told them we had been at the fair and were headed home to Oak Bluffs. Jim and I looked at each other and shrugged. I was disappointed but contented myself by looking out the window of this unfamiliar car, the moon now illuminating Sengekontacket Pond, and breathing in the scent of the strangers up front.

We sped along and reached Oak Bluffs in a matter of minutes, which was all the time it took to sense that I didn't want these people to know where Jim and I lived. When we reached Inkwell Beach, I leaned forward and said, "This will be fine right here."

Nobody said anything—nor did the car slow down. I wondered if perhaps I had done it wrong, the way to let someone know you were ready to get out.

"We would like to get out now," I said. "Right here is great."

The car slowed a bit as we entered Oak Bluffs but picked up speed as we rounded the harbor. I asked again to be let out. *Silence.* I asked again. *Silence.* I asked again and again, my voice growing quieter and more timid with each request. Jim may have spoken, too, but time has erased such details from my memory of the evening. What remains, though, so vividly that my breath quickens when I think too deeply about that night, is the fear I felt. This sort of thing only happened in the movies, I thought, or to people in a newspaper article so removed from my life as to be fictional. I prayed it was just some sort of joke, a Saturday-night joyride to scare the hell out of some kids.

I moved closer to my brother until I was pressed against his body, my hand in his. We drove toward Vineyard Haven, then turned back to a wooded area in Oak Bluffs. Up ahead on the left was a graveyard, the same one some of our island ancestors were buried in. Jim and I had explored the grounds many times on our bikes, checking out the old headstones.

I climbed into Jim's lap, trying to take shelter in the curve of his body as I begged silently for the car not to turn into the graveyard. Then the car took the turn so hard that it threw me back against the door on the side opposite Jim.

Near the graveyard's entrance stands a statue of Jesus, his arms open and welcoming. The driver circled it three times and the force continued to pin me against the door. Eventually, the car straightened out and tore down a dirt road that led deep into the woods.

Later, Jim told me that from his vantage point he could see the tall man in the front passenger seat reach for his door handle as if preparing to jump out and capture us. Perhaps they had some signal up front. In the backseat we had no time for signals: my brother simply opened his own door and jumped.

For a moment, I found myself alone in the backseat. Then the tall man spun around and reached for me. I ducked down into the foot well, crawled to the open door, and leaped into the night. When I hit the ground, I rolled in the dirt to the edge of the woods.

When I stopped rolling and could stand, I looked around and saw a light in the distance. I could hear the car skidding behind me on the dirt road, gravel kicking up, and I started running toward the light. There was no path, just blind running. Branches scratched at me, and I tripped on a root. I had no idea if the tall man had left the car to chase me.

Eventually, the woods gave way to a small clearing and a house. People stood around a keg and looked startled as I burst into the yard. I turned around and screamed for my brother.

"Jim," I yelled over and over. "Jim, it's a house."

I heard noises coming from the woods and finally he appeared, running fast and not stopping until he was snagged by a clothesline. He landed on his back, and I ran to him and knelt. A crowd quickly formed.

"What the hell is going on?" someone asked.

As our hearts pounded in our ears, we realized we knew some of the teenagers and twenty-somethings at that party—

they were friends of our older cousins. We breathlessly tried to explain what had happened and a group of the young men ran toward the graveyard. The car's headlights continued to search through the trees but then vanished before the men could reach them. The would-be kidnappers were never found.

It took my brother and me two decades to finally speak about that night. I had thought about the night often and sometimes wondered about my brother jumping out first and leaving me behind. But if he hadn't acted by opening the door and jumping, what then?

When we finally talked about it as grown men, I tried to lighten the conversation by teasing him for staying on the dirt road in the graveyard, which I thought was a stupid thing to do because they could try to run him over. I had done the smart thing, I insisted, and run off into the woods.

Jim looked at me incredulously: "I was looking for you," he said. "There was no way I was leaving that graveyard without you."

10.

THE CALL CAME when I was at work. Cathlin was crying on the other end of the line, and her small sobs made it difficult to hear her. The *Gazette* doesn't have a crowded office, but an open newsroom often carries with it several simultaneous conversations. Most of my colleagues were twenty-somethings, and I didn't want to subject them to the discussion of a married couple during a moment of sadness.

I walked outside and sat down on a small wooden bench where the smokers from the office would congregate.

"The doctor found a lump in my breast," Cathlin said.

I didn't know how to respond. I looked blankly across the street to the Charlotte Inn, a place of rarified beauty so expensive it might as well have a moat wrapped around it.

"The doctor said the biopsy will give us the news one hundred percent, but she's pretty sure it's a cancer lump," she said between sobs. "We have an appointment at Mass General next week."

I prided myself on being able to face problems with a handy to-do list: we write out the scenario, check all the boxes as we go along, and by the end of the list everything has been fixed. But the word *cancer* didn't fit on any checklist I'd ever imagined. Cancer to me meant one thing and one thing only: death. I wasn't yet a part of the armies of people who march in solidarity with cancer survivors, sharing horror stories that end in messages of hope. No. Everyone I had ever known with cancer had died: grandparents, Cathlin's mother, a fifth-grade teacher, the people in the *Gazette* obituaries I edited each week.

"I'm coming right home," I said.

"It's time to pick up the kids from school," she said.

"Oh yeah. I'll get them."

To PICK UP our kids was to do a loop around much of the island. I started by driving west from work in Edgartown to Chilmark to pick up Pickle at preschool. Some people referred to her preschool as the Chilmark School for the Blond; Pickle has curly brown hair, and her teachers both had dark hair, too, but as a whole it could have been a school for elves and fairies.

After picking up Pickle, I strapped her into the car seat and we headed northeast, back down-island to get Hardy, then a second grader at the Public Charter School, which is within walking distance of our house.

On the drive, I was quiet. *It will turn out to be nothing,* I assured myself. I glanced at Pickle in the rearview mirror.

"How was school today?" I asked.

"Good," she said cheerily. "Bobby peed his pants. But he didn't cry. I held his hand."

In a parent-teacher conference, Pickle's teachers described her as a sort of human Switzerland, a neutral territory the kids went to when feeling sad or picked on by another child. Pickle looks like me, but she has Cathlin's selfless soul. I often wish she could have known Cathlin's mother, Helen

Baker, so she could go back at least one more generation in the line of strong and thoughtful Baker women. Helen died of cancer in her early sixties, a fact I knew must have been weighing on Cathlin.

When we arrived at Hardy's school, Pickle and I walked in holding hands. The hallways were lined with books rather than lockers, and kids wandered freely about. The atmosphere was so different from the usual hallway ghost town of most schools, where a kid might be seen darting like a skittish mouse from a classroom to the bathroom. This feeling of ease is what made us choose the school.

Waiting outside Hardy's door for dismissal, I called my mother and asked if she could babysit the kids later.

"It's a bit of an emergency," I said. "I'll explain later."

"I'll be there," she said, without pressing me for more.

My parents had retired to the Vineyard just a few months earlier, more members of the clan returning to the island that for a couple of centuries our family once called home. I said a silent prayer that they were here, rather than back in New Jersey. Then I stood in the hallway, holding my daughter's hand and waiting to hold my son's, too.

THAT EVENING, CATHLIN and I drove to a restaurant, traveling to one of the down-island towns that serves alcohol. It was late fall, and the place was quiet. We ordered martinis and got out our pads and pencils. We weren't there to wonder about the possibilities or imagine a dark future. We weren't even there to hug or cry. We were there to work.

Cathlin is a planner, her skills in this arena honed as a grassroots organizer, her life before becoming a minister. I may have been a latent planner myself, an organizational wizard buried beneath layers of male ineptitude, but acquired my skills later in life thanks to Cathlin.

We placed our pads and calendars in front of us and jumped right in. But to where?

Neither of us had any idea what to expect beyond the moment we were sitting in.

The day before, our biggest worries were the morning rush to get the kids to school and the dinner and bedtime routines at the end of the day. Everything else mostly took care of itself. The kids consumed all our attention. But at the table, it was just the two of us. Date night, something we never got around to, had arrived suddenly and with a dark shadow.

We began writing, questions mostly.

What does our health insurance look like?

Where will we stay in Boston if we need to do overnights at the hospital?

Who do we call at the Steamship Authority for last-minute ferry reservations?

Who will we talk to for advice?

When and how should we tell the kids, my parents, our friends?

The list-making continued as the waiter came and went. We didn't cry or panic. Our pencils moved across the pages and made it seem as though we were, for one last fleeting moment, still in control of our lives, safe in the bubble of a restaurant filled with people eating and laughing.

Then Cathlin stopped writing and looked at me.

"How the hell am I going to write a sermon for Sunday?" she asked.

CATHLIN DID, OF course, find the strength to write a sermon for that Sunday. She did it by being open about what was happening in our lives and bringing her congregation along for the difficult journey. That was our choice, and for us it was the right choice. No matter what happened, we never felt alone.

But on that first Sunday after her diagnosis, we knew none of this. We were blindly moving forward in a way that Cathlin was able to illustrate at the end of the sermon she wrote: we were moving forward in faith—not a faith that all would be well, but a faith in love.

Our faith does not keep bad things from happening to us, but faithful stewardship of our lives, our minds and our bodies, enables us to endure the hard times, to make it through the wilderness to the other side. And so, as we sit and count our blessings, we are sifting apart the wheat and the chaff of our lives. And it is this very process that is an alchemy of sorts, for the chaff falls to the ground and we are left with the wheat, left with the spiritual food that will sustain us. And so, now nourished by this spiritual food, I turn to the refiner's fire. I plan to throw myself, my illness, and my fears into the fire where I know God's loving hands will mold me into something new, something golden, something to keep and treasure. Amen.

11.

~~~~~~

A s we drove off the ferry onto the mainland, Cathlin turned to me and said, "Don't mind me, I have an extreme sense of well-being." She then proceeded to chatter and laugh, even waving occasionally to strangers in cars beside us as we waited in traffic on our way to Boston.

Cathlin has never been a glass half-full or a glass half-empty person—she has always been a glass-overflowing kind of woman. But considering we were headed to her first chemotherapy treatment, this was a bit much even for her. In November she was diagnosed with breast cancer, stage one, curable, but already making inroads in her lymph nodes. In the first two months after diagnosis, there were two surgeries, and then it was time for chemotherapy. Later, more surgery and radiation loomed.

Her good cheer wasn't denial, but rather a side effect of the pre-chemo drugs she was taking. We laughed when we read the label on the bottle, "Warning: may cause an extreme sense of well-being," and we were laughing again. It felt good to laugh, a sound that had been in short supply since this journey began. When Cathlin first received her diagnosis, I felt disconnected and mostly in denial. I did a lot of pushups and felt the urge to go hunting, something I've never done. I considered bow hunting or, better yet, just a knife and a loincloth. The more primal the better.

Occasionally the full force of what was happening to my wife would hit me and as suddenly as a sneeze I would break down crying. Once, out walking, just the smell of a certain bush, a scent that took me back to childhood, set me off. I bawled as if I were in my room alone with the shades drawn, rather than walking the streets of Edgartown on a sunny winter morning. A FedEx man, his arms full of packages, emerged from his truck. He paused and looked at me.

"Are you okay?" he asked.

"No," I replied.

Buoyed by Cathlin's extreme sense of well-being, we navigated Boston's tangle of streets, arrived at Massachusetts General Hospital, and headed to the cancer wing. I said a silent thank-you to the Yawkey family, former owners of the Red Sox, who donated this wing. Philanthropists, doctors, and nurses were now the most important people in our lives. We passed a gift shop filled not with the normal hospital tchotchkes, cards, and stuffed animals, but a room stuffed with fluffy hats, head scarves, and wigs—yet another reminder that we were in the major leagues here.

In the waiting room, an old man was pushing around a cart loaded with snacks and water. He asked everyone "How are you?" and within each cluster of people determined who was the patient.

"God bless you," he told each one in turn. "I hope everything goes well."

Later, while Cathlin had her blood drawn and vitals checked, I walked down the hallway. Tibetan prayer flags hung from the ceiling, each one inscribed with the hopeful words of a loved one: STAY STRONG MOM; I LOVE DAD; GOD HELP US; and my favorite, BRING IT ON.

I entered the Resource Room, which I had been told was a great place to find all manner of books to help me deal with what we were going through. Mostly, though, I found a new vocabulary. Not that I didn't know what the word cancer meant, but now it was so much more real and no longer an abstraction, like a mythical bogeyman lurking far off stage. I scanned the rows of books and noticed one called *Home Before Dark*, which sounded promising, but then decided the Resource Room was not for me when I encountered another titled *When the Sun Goes Down*.

Some have the luxury of dealing with cancer on their own, but because Cathlin is a minister, we had to go public quite early. I was thankful for this. Neighbors delivered so many delicious meals for us that I began to feel as if I had forgotten how to cook dinner. The dinners were just one of many gifts showered upon us—the church ladies were soon baking us pot brownies and cookies and leaving them on our doorstep.

Before we told the community, we had to make sure Hardy and Pickle were fully aware of what was happening to Mommy.

When we told Hardy we wanted to talk with him, he edged to the far side of the room, suspecting he was in trouble. He digested the news quickly—the word *cancer* not holding for him the same ring of finality it held for earlier generations—and immediately reached for his crayons and a piece of paper. He drew a battle scene with numerous bad-guy cells and a ray gun destroying them; oddly enough, they all had mustaches. Then Hardy quickly asked to be excused to play in his tree house.

Pickle responded to the news by beginning to talk a lot about taking a trip to outer space.

After Cathlin's lab work was studied to make sure her white blood cell count was sufficient, we were shuttled into the infusion room. There were three other patients in our wing, all regulars it seemed, as we were the only ones to receive the welcome talk and an explanation about what was about to happen and what to expect in the coming days. Everyone, from the doctors to the nurses to the receptionists, was so patient and kind that our feelings toward them went beyond just liking and appreciation: we wanted to take them home with us.

One of the patients was a pregnant woman who wore a fluffy hat; a sign that her hair had already fallen out. Her husband sat next to her, working at his computer. They had the routine down.

An older man sat in the far corner talking to a woman I assumed was his wife. The man looked like the French actor Gerard Depardieu. He also looked incredibly healthy and had a full head of hair. That's the thing about cancer patients in the early stages: outwardly someone with a minor cold might look sicker.

The other woman was alone, with no one at her bedside.

At first there was only minimal contact with our neighbors. Shy smiles, mostly. But as the long afternoon progressed—it would take almost four hours to administer all the bags of chemicals via an IV drip—there was small talk. Later, a magnificent sunset flooded the room with a startling array of colors and those who could, mostly the caregivers and nurses, stood together at the window marveling at the beauty of the moment.

Back on the island, when people stopped to ask me how I was doing, some would say they thought the spouse of a cancer patient had it hardest. I was tired and scared, but I disagreed. Frustration was constant, an extension of the exhaustion and helplessness that came with not being able to make someone you love feel better. But this didn't even begin to compare with what Cathlin faced. Often, I would notice her sitting on the couch and staring off into the distance, something she never did before. She was, I suspect, confronting the very nature of our fragile and finite existence. She also had to surmount the physical challenges alone, from the side effects of chemotherapy (the other drugs didn't provide the same warm bubble of extreme well-being) to the reality of the changes her body was undergoing.

When our nurse declared there was about forty-five minutes left for the last bag of chemicals, I walked outside and down the block to make a reservation at a fancy restaurant near the hospital. Cathlin had about thirty-six hours before she would start feeling sick from the effects of the chemo, so I wanted her to enjoy a special meal. But the woman at the front desk shook her head when I asked about tables and told me they were full for the evening. I nodded slowly, silent. Perhaps she sensed something because she asked, "Are you celebrating anything special tonight?"

"The end of my wife's first chemotherapy infusion," I said.

The woman, who I later learned was a nurse in training, looked away briefly, then turned back to me and said, "There will be a table waiting for whatever time you choose, sir."

A FEW WEEKS after her first infusion, Cathlin's hair fell out in large clumps. The children took the hair into the backyard as an offering to the birds for their nests. Then I drove Cathlin down the road not far from where we lived to Patti Linn's salon to get her head shaved. I stood by her side the whole time and when the shears quieted and we encountered this new person looking back at us in the mirror, I blurted out, "Beautiful." And I meant it sincerely: her bare head drew attention to her bright blue eyes. And her smile, wide under normal circumstances, seemed even wider.

"Beautiful," I said again.

But there were no drugs that morning offering an extreme sense of well-being, and I could tell Cathlin didn't believe me.

12.

⁓⁓⁓

I N THE DAYS following chemotherapy, the family bedtime routines shifted for all of us in different ways. Sometimes Pickle and I would lie in her bed and talk, about the day that had ended or the one to come. Other times, we were quiet and I would simply kneel at her bedside and scratch her back until she fell asleep.

One night, after she nodded off, I slowly eased out of her bedroom, crawling on my hands and knees across the floor to muffle my sound on the carpet. Along the way I encountered a maze of stuffed animals, which I gently moved out of the way to create a path to the doorway. When I reached the hall, I stood up and peeked my head into Hardy's room. He was asleep, lying on his back in a tangle of blankets, as if he had run a long race in his dreams. I stepped into his room and stood there for a moment, watching him breathe.

When Hardy was born, there were complications. Cathlin chose to have a natural delivery, with no anesthesia. During the delivery, she incurred a large tear and had to be rushed out of the birthing room to a surgical room with more equipment. One nurse wheeled her out and another handed Hardy to me, saying, "Here you go, Dad."

I stood in the birthing room alone, holding my first-born child, expecting someone to come back and tell me what to do. I waited but no one came. Finally, I sat in a wooden rocker, holding Hardy and staring at his small pink face. He had entered the world screaming, his arms rigid and his fingers outstretched like jazz hands, but now he was calm. I rocked and I cried, holding my son. I never really knew what I wanted to be when I grew up, what job I wanted to do or places I wanted to see. But I had always known one thing I wanted for my future: I wanted to be a father. I knew this even as a small child. I never wondered about it, found it odd, or did anything to prepare for it. On the contrary—much of my life seemed to be spent delaying it; I was forty when Hardy was born.

I straightened Hardy's blankets and covered him, then placed my hand on his forehead, heavy enough for him to feel it but light enough so I didn't wake him. Then I continued down the hall on my nightly rounds and checked on Cathlin. She was lying in bed with her eyes closed but not asleep. Earlier in the evening, the children and I placed a small garbage can next to her side of the bed in case she needed to throw up, but the anti-nausea pills seemed to be working. Instead of her throwing up, the chemotherapy had resulted in more of a general weakening and a journey to some half state, neither here nor fully somewhere else. Cathlin looked gray and for three days she stayed that way, not eating or doing much of anything else, and then gradually she returned to us—and we would have an almost normal two weeks until the cycle repeated itself.

I looked at Cathlin lying in our bed, her chest slowly rising and falling, and thought, *No, the story of my family does not end here.* When she first received the diagnosis, we visited another couple who had traveled this road. In addition to some general advice, they said, "This will be the worst year of your life . . . but then it will be over, and you'll be okay." I forced myself to believe them.

I rested my palm on Cathlin's head, lightly but firmly, as I had with Hardy, to let her know I was there, but also to transmit to her that she didn't need to do anything. She did not need to open her eyes or smile or try to reassure me that everything would be okay. All her life she has been the one to help others. As a minister, she often sits with people in pain, both physically and emotionally. But unlike a doctor, she doesn't offer solutions. Instead, she offers herself.

After a few minutes I left the room, walked downstairs, and headed outside. My feet were bare even though it was January and very cold. I looked up at the sky, which was so clear it seemed to reveal everything. A sliver of moon lit a path across our yard and into the dark woods. But I didn't choose to travel that way. Instead, I dropped down on all fours, and while my son and daughter slept and my wife tossed and turned, I did pushups on the porch. As I exercised, I watched my breath leave my body in thick clouds until I finally collapsed and turned over onto my back to look up at the sky once again. It was filled with stars, and as I stared at them, I felt myself shrinking, becoming small and insignificant. Oddly enough, I found this comforting.

13.

⁓

WHEN CATHLIN AND I were married, in 2001 at Judson Memorial Church in New York City, the ceremony was part tradition and part theater. Cathlin wore a red dress and we walked down the aisle together, entering the church already as a couple.

About halfway through the service, a very tall man stood up in the back row and began waving his arms and yelling, "Wait. Wait. What about the objections part? What about giving our reasons why this couple can't get married?"

Everyone turned in horror. My mother, seated in the front row, went white.

The man left his seat and made his way up the aisle, still ranting about objections. He approached us at the altar and then, after giving us a wink, he turned to face the congregation.

"Isn't that a silly tradition," our friend Paul said. "How about we flip it and instead give reasons why this couple *should* get married."

For the next ten minutes, friends and family stood and testified to why Cathlin and I were made for each other. The reasons varied from "You're both short!" to "You both look great in a red dress!" But mostly it came down to how well we complemented each other.

A decade later, we celebrated our tenth wedding anniversary by leaving the kids with relatives and going back to New York City. We stayed at the Washington Square Hotel, just a few blocks from Judson Church, and attended services there. Seated once again in that beautiful space I thought back to our wedding day, the overwhelming joy of it and especially that moment when Paul surprised our loved ones and in response they publicly embraced us.

On our anniversary, it never crossed my mind to recall a different moment in the service: "I take you Cathlin to be my wife, in sickness and in health."

A wedding day feels far removed from disease or any misfortune. Even ninety-two-year-old great-grandpa is doing the chicken dance with the six-year-old flower girl. Everyone present has spirit and vitality, and nobody more so than the bride and groom. However, not only does the reality of aging await us all, so too do the seemingly inevitable battles with disease.

SEVEN MONTHS PAST the day of Cathlin's cancer diagnosis the prognosis remained quite good and her doctors were pleased with the journey so far. There had been many surgeries and sessions of chemotherapy. Only radiation remained.

When anyone asked me how we were doing, I always answered that it had been a tough slog, which it had been. And yet, there were moments of beauty, too. Take date night, that mythical nirvana held dear by parents of small children everywhere. For years we were too busy or too tired, the kids too sick or a babysitter too hard to find—it was always something. Chemotherapy weekends, on the other hand, we never missed.

Every three weeks during Cathlin's treatment, we traveled to Boston, just the two of us, and after she received her infusion of chemicals stayed for the weekend. The after-effects would not completely take over for forty-eight hours, so we had time to truly be together before Cathlin left us—my term for what chemo did, turning her into more of a ghostly presence laid out in bed or on the couch than a wife or mother.

In Boston, each moment had a heightened clarity, whether signing a health care proxy or watching bad TV in a hotel room. Sure, I would have welcomed the ephemeral moments of dinner or a movie, but now my heart held unique memories that have reverberated through my life, like Cathlin praying over her chemotherapy drugs—"Sending them my love"—while her oncology nurse, Samantha, and I bowed our heads and stood silently next to her.

Or when we made our way to the Salon at 10 Newbury to meet with the owner, Patricia Wrixon, who for more than three decades had been making wigs for cancer patients and transgender clients. We walked through the front room, a huge loft with glass windows looking out onto Newbury Street, and passed the regular patrons getting ready for dates, weddings, or just receiving their monthly spruce-up. Everyone seemed impossibly beautiful as we were guided to the back room, where there would be no windows and the doors remained closed. While it seemed at first that we had been shunted to the margins, the tenderness shown to us in that room, from both Patricia and the stylist who joined us and told us the story of her own mother's struggle with breast

cancer, made it seem as if this really was the place we wanted to be—actually, *wanted* is not the right word, because we
would have wanted anything but to experience Cathlin's illness, but I can't deny being brought to a place of feeling I
had never known before. When Cathlin worked as a hospice
chaplain, she would tell me that no matter what else happened in her day, she knew she was doing the most important thing possible at that moment. Being a caregiver was like
that for me, too, bringing with it a clarity and focus that were
grounding—the fragility of our lives then made our bond feel
stronger. Our journey from knowing each other as teenagers,
to the freedom of our twenty-something lives, to a place of
needing each other just to make it through the day, put our
love on a higher plane.

Another memory. After Cathlin's double mastectomy,
when she couldn't raise her arms above her waist, I'd take
the kids to school each morning and then return to the
house to help her bathe. I sat on a light blue IKEA stool beside the bathtub, just as I did when washing the children,
while Cathlin tried to find a comfortable position, leaning
forward to receive the full breadth of the warm washcloth
on her shoulders. After a moment, she'd lift her head and I'd
massage her bare scalp, shampooing the skin and rinsing her
head with cupsful of water.

This daily baptism was for us alone, no children or other
family present.

Cathlin's baldness was near total. Only a few especially
tough hairs remained, including one extremely long one,
about four inches, that continued to blossom just above her
forehead. It was so slight as to be almost hidden. Each night,
the children would play a modified version of Where's Wal-

do?, refusing to go to bed until they had found and stroked this one elongated and somehow elegant hair.

We remained open with Hardy and Pickle during every step of Cathlin's journey, and it was the right decision for our family. Yet, being open—especially with kids—didn't lead in a single direction that simply embraced the difficulties and came out the other side stronger. Children have a way of revealing how life often chooses a punch in the gut to a fair fight.

During the run-up to her fourth birthday, Pickle told us she didn't want to have a party. In fact, she didn't want anyone to take notice of the day, whatsoever. When we traveled into Boston for chemotherapy appointments, Cathlin's sister, Cecilia, drove up from New Jersey to stay with the kids so they could sleep in their own beds and maintain some level of normalcy. Pickle finally confided to Cecilia why she didn't want to celebrate her birthday.

"Pickle is convinced she'll die when she turns four," Cecilia told us over the phone. "She says four is old and that's what happens when you get old."

A week later, during the end of our nighttime routine, Pickle turned to me. The room was relatively dark, just the glow from her butterfly nightlight highlighting us lying together in her bed. We managed to share her tiny pillow as we read books. Above us, her bower, not unlike a cascade of mosquito netting, gave the sense of being cocooned away from the rest of the world: just the two of us floating safely in a scrim of white.

"When will I die?" Pickle asked me.

"I don't know," I said.

"Before you?"

"That's not the way it usually works," I hedged.

"Dada . . . I want to die before you. That way, I won't have to miss you."

I wanted to tell Pickle that she would never die, that she and I and Mommy and Hardy would live forever and never have to face sadness or illness. But, of course, I couldn't. And so I said nothing and just hugged her tightly until she fell asleep.

LATER, SITTING BY myself in the dark, I thought back to our wedding day and that moment when our loved ones stood and testified before Cathlin and me.

There are so many reasons why Cathlin and I married. Many I can articulate easily. Others are beyond words—they float in front of me every night, carried in the blood and breath of our children.

14.

~~~

MARTHA'S VINEYARD IS a forty-five-minute ferry ride and then a ninety-mile drive to Boston, so we hadn't visited the city often. But during chemotherapy we traveled there every few weeks. All Cathlin saw of the city was Massachusetts General Hospital, but during her long infusions I would sometimes take a break and wander the streets.

I enjoyed the feeling of anonymity a city is so expert at delivering. On the Vineyard, especially in the off-season, everything is familiar—every road and every face. Walking around Boston, I could feel myself disappear, which was exactly what I wanted.

I roamed by chance, turning left or right and experiencing the rush of being shoulder to shoulder with humanity, letting the smells and sounds wash over me. I sat in cafés, hunched over my coffee, looking out at the other lives, eavesdropping on conversations as I had for years in New York— or "ears dropping," as Pickle called it when we did it together, each of us sitting and listening and smiling and then comparing notes on the stories we overheard.

One day I wandered into a bookstore, and while browsing came upon a row of books by Donald Hall. Years ago, Cathlin and I read Hall's memoir of his childhood, String Too Short to Be Saved, and loved it. I pulled down two books of his that chronicle the death of his wife, the poet Jane Kenyon, from leukemia. One book—*The Best Day the Worst Day*—is prose, the other—*Without*—poetry. I purchased both.

At home, I hid the Hall books near my bedside table, deep under a pile of other books. They are books of love and devotion but without happy endings. Hall writes unflinchingly about his wife's illness as they marched toward her death, and I didn't want Cathlin to see me reading his books—I didn't want her to think I had lost hope.

I never lost hope.

But I wanted a companion, someone who had walked this treacherous road and didn't look away. All my life I'd been told to look on the bright side, to cross the street when bad news approached. But I refused to ignore so much as a second of Cathlin's illness. I wanted to feel every moment, no matter how difficult.

Donald Hall helped me do this, reading him late at night when Cathlin and the kids were fast asleep. He held my hand and taught me how to feel not only deeply but with my eyes wide open, too.

15.

~~~

FOR MOST OF the six weeks of her radiation treatment, Cathlin stayed at a friend's apartment in Boston. During her surgeries and chemotherapy, I was with her for each step, sitting with her as bags of chemicals slowly made their way into her body via an intravenous drip, or walking with her down the hospital corridors and holding her hand until we finally came to a line on the floor demarcating the operating room, where I could go no farther.

But for radiation, Cathlin traveled mostly alone while I held down the logistical house of cards back on the island. Radiation is a daily thirty-minute zap and gradually the zaps and exhaustion add up. Piling on a daily commute from the island would have been too much.

When Cathlin called me each evening, she always shared stories about the friends she made. Cathlin has what one personality test described as a very high *Woo*, or "win-others-over," trait. When she enters a room, she leads with her infectious smile, something so real it feels rare and precious and you're not so much drawn to it as relaxed by it.

Because she was accepted into a study of women diagnosed with breast cancer at an early age (forty-three) and whose cancer was on the left side, nearer the heart, she was treated by a proton laser rather than a photon one. The proton machine is much more exact and able to pinpoint the lasers precisely so not as much skin is affected. This kind of energy doesn't go as deeply into the body, thus keeping the heart safer. There were only ten such cyclotrons in use in the United States at the time and usually they're reserved for brain cancer and all manner of pediatric cases.

When the doctor told us about the study and the proton laser, we thought, "Great, a bigger and better machine!" But it also meant that Cathlin's peer group, the people she saw every day at radiation, were not those with a good chance of survival. Her friends were patients with cases far more complicated and with a much less favorable prognosis. Her closest companion was a heart surgeon with a rare form of spinal cancer. Thankfully, she shielded me from stories about the children she sat with in the waiting room.

FOR CATHLIN'S LAST day of radiation treatment, the kids and I drove into Boston to be with her.

Pickle decided to dress as the hobbit Frodo Baggins. Her costume consisted of a pair of blue jeans, a white mesh shirt she said was woven from the elven material *mithril*, and a long turquoise cape. As Frodo was often dirty during his quest to Mordor, she insisted that her face be rubbed with mud.

Hardy wore the same pants and shirt he had worn nearly every day for the past few months. Making him change his clothes was just one of many things I stopped worrying about.

After buckling in the kids, I sat in the driver's seat and asked what song we should play to mark this momentous occasion.

"'Psycho Killer!'" Hardy shouted.

The kids and I had been listening to an old CD compilation of punk and new wave songs I found in a box in the basement. The collection of tunes by the Sex Pistols, Blondie, Elvis Costello, and the Talking Heads buoyed our mood. We were a raucous group and when we drove, we played the CD music very loud.

"'Gloria!'" Pickle suggested after I said "Psycho Killer" might not be appropriate for the moment. She waved her sword in the air, and with her flock of corkscrew curls she did indeed look like a hobbit.

"Perfect," I said in response to the Patti Smith anthem. We pulled out of our driveway, heading down-island to pick up my mother and Cathlin's sister and then to the ferry. For a moment, it felt like a family road trip with music and snacks and head-banging tunes. The end of this cancer treatment was near and I couldn't believe we had made it through, changed but still whole.

After a few miles, Pickle called to me from the backseat. I turned the music down.

"What is it, Pickle?"

"Did Patti Smith die of cancer?" she asked.

WE ARRIVED IN Boston in the late afternoon. The last radiation appointment was set for 1:00 p.m. the next day.

That night, we ordered Chinese food and set up sleeping arrangements for the kids. We talked about the last treatment, and there was a celebratory atmosphere in the room. But for me the euphoria of the drive to Boston gave way to something else. Not a quiet reflectiveness, but something much more unsteady.

In the morning I found it difficult to breathe and took Pickle in search of good coffee. She was only part Frodo with a cape but no dirt smudges or sword stick; we were in the city, after all. We found a perfect café near the Boston Common.

Afterwards, walking back through the Common with Pickle on my shoulders, we came upon an ancient graveyard. There was a fence circling it, and the headstones were both crumbling and majestic. Pickle and I watched as a hawk landed on one of the larger headstones and began to preen himself. He cocked his head and looked directly at us. The moment was arresting and yet so peaceful and beautiful that I found myself relaxing for the first time since we'd left the Vineyard. A wave of confusion washed over me: We had looked forward to this day for so long and now, when it finally arrived, I wanted no part of it.

We left the apartment early with plenty of time to make it to the hospital. We didn't want to be late for the last day and we also wanted to seek out some fun for the kids. There's a carousel and a bit of an urban water park in the middle of the Common, a mostly macadam area the size of a football field filled with shin-high water and a few fountains. It was a hot July day, and after a carousel ride the kids changed into their bathing suits.

Hardy began to act up, scaring his sister and being a general nuisance. I asked him to walk with me, and we moved about twenty yards away to have a talk. Sometime during the cancer journey, I learned I could no longer even raise my voice with my children, and instead we began to have hushed talks. I wish I could say this was because the experience of my wife's cancer made me a more empathic soul and able to deal with difficult situations in an enlightened way. But that's not it at all. I had to stop yelling because I scared myself.

One day, Hardy had become very frustrated before school. His favorite pants were too dirty to wear, and he threw a tantrum, something that would have been annoying when he was four, but at age seven his behavior struck me as so wrong that it was clear my son would grow up to be a horrible person.

So I yelled. I yelled a lot.

But my yelling only added to the commotion and Hardy cried louder. When we finally made it to the car, he was still crying and I was still yelling. When we approached the school, I decided we couldn't arrive in this state so I kept driving. I had no plan, I just drove.

After a bit, Hardy stopped crying and asked me where we were going. He seemed frightened. The anger he had been expressing minutes before had been replaced by a slight tremor in his voice. I didn't say anything. I just kept driving, getting some sick sense of enjoyment out of my son's repeated pleas to know where we were going.

We drove on far too long, my silence in the front seat and my son's fearful questions coming from the back.

Eventually, I turned the car around.

We drove home rather than to school, walked inside the house, and sat on the couch, side by side. My adrenaline was still high from my anger, but more so because I had frightened myself. I had become my son's torturer, even enjoying how much I scared him.

I apologized to Hardy and then we talked quietly.

"When something bad happens," Hardy said, "I don't only think about that thing. I think about every bad thing that has ever happened or will happen. That's why I can't stop the tantrum."

I thought about my anger at my son, how it had little to do with the moment and everything to do with all the other bad things that were happening. How Hardy and I each buckled under the weight of life's stresses was, I realized, not dissimilar.

I could only make it through each day covered in an armor of scheduling. I compiled lists of phone numbers of relatives, friends, and babysitters, and created flow charts detailing where the kids would be each day and with whom. I fed them and dressed them and put them to bed, trying for the most part to keep them happy and as walled off from their mother's cancer as best as possible. And then, in the early morning before they woke, I sat alone in the predawn dark with my coffee and discovered new ways to cry.

AT MASSACHUSETTS GENERAL Hospital, we took the elevator down five flights to the basement. When the doors opened and we walked out, we were greeted like celebrities.

"You get to ring the bell today, right?" a man asked Hardy. He nodded and smiled.

The bell was a last-day-of-radiation tradition. It hung from the wall not too far from the elevators. Above the bell was a large CONGRATULATIONS! sign. Below it were the words: WHEN MY TREATMENTS ARE DONE, THIS BELL MUST BE RUNG.

A nurse led us out of the waiting room and down several twisty corridors.

"Radiation doesn't like corners," he told us.

We were all following him: the kids, my mother, Cathlin's sister, Cecilia, and Cathlin, changed into her gown, booties, and head wrap. Before radiation began, she received five small blue tattoos, permanent dots on her body to help align where the radiation would be pinpointed. I could see two of these blue dots, one just above her sternum, the other by her shoulder.

When we finally reached the cyclotron, I was amazed by its size. It took up most of the room, a hulking machine that could accommodate three people at a time, each one listening to their favorite piped-in music. "The machine weighs a hundred tons," the nurse told us, "and is three stories tall."

After a few minutes of exploring and making sure the kids didn't fall off the edge of the floor, we all hugged Cathlin—we hugged the nurses and technicians, too. Then we walked slowly back to the waiting room.

My mother and Cecilia took Pickle upstairs to buy flowers. Hardy befriended a boy whose mom was also being treated for breast cancer and they found a computer in the children's room and played video games. I took a seat in the waiting room next to a mother and father and their little girl, who was perhaps ten years old. She had crutches and wore a thick wool hat to hide her baldness.

I looked up when the elevator dinged, and a new family stepped out. A boy led the group. He wore a Little League uniform with his cap pulled down low, but it couldn't cover as much as the girl's wool hat.

Another family arrived and I immediately scanned the children's heads. There were three of them, but everyone had a full head of hair. Then I saw they were carrying a large chocolate cake. One of the nurses ran out from behind her desk and approached the oldest boy, who looked to be in his early teens.

"Oh, you look so good," she gushed. "And grown up!"

"Yes, he got his hair back," the mother said. "It makes him look older."

The boy smiled with no trace of the shyness or awkwardness around adults that kids his age usually display. He carried the cake to the reception desk and passed plates around to all the nurses and staff. I couldn't tell if it was a checkup with his oncologist or an anniversary party, maybe commemorating one year after his last treatment. In any case, the boy looked healthy, as if nothing had ever happened to him. I felt so happy for him, but worried about him, too.

Everybody returned to the waiting room, and my thoughts returned to my wife and children.

Suddenly, Cathlin walked into the room, and we all let out a cheer. We gathered around her, and we made our way to the bell. But I found myself drifting to the edge of the group.

I lived in New York City during 9/11. I still remember the day very clearly, the chaos, fear, and sadness hovering in the smoke-filled the streets. People were on high alert and talking to one another, even the normal barrier of strangers on the subway suddenly lifted. But not for me. I learned on that day, among other things, that when emotions run so high, it's as though the brakes have failed on one's internal thermometer and I shut down and click into survival mode.

I can execute tasks with a heightened clarity, but all feeling goes fuzzy, almost as if my heart has been placed in a safe house in order for my mind to function.

That's how I felt in Boston.

The others stepped up to the ceremonial bell and rang it. First Hardy, then Pickle, and then Cathlin. The nurses clapped and cheered. Cecilia cried and my mother embraced her. But I hovered in the background, wanting desperately to be alone, perhaps reading a book in my childhood bed, covered in my football sheets and looking at the posters on the wall of my hero at the time, the Lakota leader Crazy Horse.

AFTER WE RETURNED home, I continued to drift in a sort of semi-darkness. The initial feeling of being unplugged worsened, as I also felt guilty for not being able to celebrate. It was over: no more surgeries, chemotherapy, or radiation. I fully believed this. And yet I could barely smile. It's as impossible to describe now as it was to comprehend then.

One night, Cathlin told me she had read about post-traumatic stress disorder being common in caregivers of cancer patients. It made a lot of sense—but knowing it didn't provide me with the ladder I needed to climb out of the hole.

The net of semi-darkness hung over me for a long time. Gradually, I began to return to my old self. There was no single moment, only an accretion of details registering that a degree of normalcy had returned.

Getting ready for school one morning, Hardy pulled a hat out of the closet, one of Cathlin's that she'd worn to hide her baldness. He picked it up and looked at it for a moment.

"Oh, this is from when Mommy was having breast cancer," he said. He spoke out loud as if confirming to himself the news that the cancer was indeed in the past tense.

Another day, I came home from work, put my backpack down, and sat on the couch as usual. I sat quietly, staring at nothing. Then I suddenly became aware that without my noticing, Pickle had crawled into my lap. She had become so adept at this, appearing as if by magic and snuggling in so tightly, that Hardy had begun calling her a lap ninja.

I looked down at her.

"Dada," she said. "Would you like to help me find the lost unicorn and run away from cheetahs?"

I smiled. "I would like nothing better," I said.

The two of us tiptoed to the door and peered with exaggerated deliberation into the backyard looking for cheetahs. While looking outside, a flash of memory hit me. Cathlin and I were at the hospital on the way to her surgery. She had already finished chemo and was thin and bald. I pushed her through the hallways in a wheelchair and noticed how others, patients and visitors, glanced at us, looked away, and then looked back again. It was as if they were thinking, *Oh, there goes someone worse off than me or my loved ones.*

Cathlin did look bad, every bit the quintessential cancer victim. But it was in that moment that I felt a sense of peace come over me. In a way, our whole little family suffered a sort of illness as we took care of Cathlin, but we absorbed the cruel blow together. After Cathlin's surgery, Pickle chose a snuggle spot down by her mother's feet where she could disappear under the blankets. She would lie there for hours, quietly rubbing her mother's ankles and feet; for no apparent reason Pickle called this place her "jewelry box."

Hardy continuously drew pictures of ray guns shooting out the cancer cells, and wore a bright blue wig in solidarity with his mother. My sister-in-law, Cecilia, moved into our house to take care of the kids whenever we went to Boston for our chemo weekends. Cathlin's brother, Alex, and his wife, Martha, came to help after surgery. My mother and father, retired and living on the island, gave up their winter months in Florida to help us in every way imaginable. Help from our family and community was essential. But pushing Cathlin in her wheelchair through the hospital that day I was overcome by the realization that, at some point, it all came down to the two of us who had somehow managed to find one another, fall in love, start a family, and stick by each other's side. I felt as if my life—and my ability to give it over to the one I loved—really mattered.

"Hey, Dada," Pickle said, interrupting my thoughts. "Is the coast clear? See any cheetahs?"

"I don't know," I said. "But that lost unicorn needs our help."

We ran out of the house. I reached down, scooped up Pickle, and put her on my shoulders, never slowing down. As I picked up speed, I felt lighter with each stride. We were really moving. No cheetah could catch us. The unicorn was out there, and we would know it when we saw it. It was the one, Pickle said, wearing a bushy blue wig to hide its bald spot.

16.

GRADUALLY, CATHLIN'S HAIR grew back. In our first Christmas photo after her last treatment, her hair isn't much longer than a crew cut, but her smile is wide again and her eyes bright. Her energy slowly increased and bit by bit our lives returned to normal. And that may be the strangest part of the whole experience, that after a year of thinking about cancer and nothing else, we were able, for the most part, to put it on a shelf and go back to the life we had been living, as if a very messy room had been cleaned and, on the surface, looked presentable.

But, of course, we were changed. And so was our relationship to the island.

I no longer lived with one foot still in New York or wondered how many years we might stay, ebbing and flowing out at sea, before cracking under the strain of a small community. Going through cancer so publicly had anchored us.

The summer people left and the harvest festivals, full of familiar faces, returned. There were hayrides and hay mazes, pumpkin festivals and pumpkins launched by catapult. Pickle started her last year of preschool, Hardy entered third grade. At Halloween, they dressed as a gnome and baby Yoda, and the island's small year-round population converged on a single street to trick or treat. Wild turkeys appeared around every bend in the road. I eased off the accelerator, looked around with fresh eyes at our small-town life, and thought, *Yes, I can do this.*

Cathlin settled into her rhythm, too, preaching again every Sunday, taking the congregation through the Christmas story, holding the annual pageant in a barn in the center of the island. Her hair grew back, thicker and curlier than it had been before the cancer, and she stopped lying awake each night in fear. We let down our guard—sort of—and began living again.

17.

BEFORE BECOMING A parent, there are so many things you don't know. The big-ticket items are all unknowns—not only *How will I afford this?* but also *Am I ready to give up my freedom?* You may understand that there will be sleepless nights, but you have no idea how truly torturous it can become.

And if you think about your future children and school at all, it's about education. The idea that school drop-off will rule your life isn't even on the radar. And yet those moments in the car on your daily drive or huddled together with other parents on the outskirts of the playground become, in a way, the benchmarks of each day.

During Cathlin's cancer treatments, I became the morning drop-off guy. Hardy's school was only a short bike ride away, but Pickle's preschool was a twenty-minute drive to Chilmark. It was just the two of us in the car each day, and it quickly became a musical experience of sorts, with no censors or suggestions of what was appropriate.

Pickle fell in step with my groove early on, leaning heavily toward male musicians of the late 1970s. In our hermetically sealed musical education chamber—a Honda Fit—one could say she had no choice. But if a three-year-old isn't willing to hear Townes Van Zandt sing about lost love and too much drink and would rather be soothed by Raffi or Barney, she can make life miserable for the man at the wheel.

On the occasion of her last day of preschool, Pickle chose Springsteen's album *Darkness on the Edge of Town*, track five in particular: "Racing in the Streets." It was the most-played song for years on our daily commute.

Until we were in the car that morning, I hadn't given much thought to Pickle's last day of preschool. But after just three beats into Bruce's song, I began to cry.

I snuck looks at Pickle in the backseat but this only increased my sniveling. My daughter was wearing her older brother's baseball cap and her long curls cascaded around her shoulders. When she started preschool, she didn't have much hair at all—a baseball cap would have covered every strand.

Pickle appeared unaffected by the moment.

As the drive continued, I thought back to earlier days when we played a lot of Joe Strummer, beginning with his career fronting the 101ers before he made it big with the Clash and on to his time with the Mescaleros. During one of our drives, I told Pickle how sad I was the day I heard Joe had died of a congenital heart defect at the age of just fifty.

"Is everyone who sings in the car dead?" she asked.

Pickle had just started preschool when Cathlin's breast cancer ordeal began. Punk rock got us through. The Sex Pistols, the Clash, the Velvet Underground, but mostly Patti Smith, helped give voice to our sadness and frustration that year. No matter what we encountered at home with Cathlin on the couch suffering the effects of chemotherapy and radiation, we knew the ride to school would be filled with singing and shouting, and the occasional naughty word. I heard later that during those days Pickle was an exceptionally energetic member of circle time.

After Cathlin had recovered, I tried some Bob Marley and Jimmy Cliff on the morning commute, but Pickle shook her head at the relaxed reggae vibe. She wanted more Springsteen.

We'd started with the *Seeger Sessions*, an album of classic folk songs Springsteen infused with rock and roll energy. Eventually, we found our way to *Darkness on the Edge of Town*, or as Pickle liked to say, "Young Bruce." She always referred to "Racing in the Streets" as "the sad song." The tone and quiet piano set the mood, but it was the line "She sits on the porch of her daddy's house / but all her pretty dreams are torn" that seemed to strike her the deepest.

"Why is she so sad?" she asked me one morning. I thought for a moment, trying to hear Springsteen's songs from a little girl's perspective. His anthems to young men seeking glory and the open road took a sharp turn for me. The women in his songs always seem to get a raw deal, mostly because they just sit around waiting while the guys chase their dreams.

"Well, Pickle," I said, "I think she's sad because she was hoping for something, but it didn't come true."

Pickle put her thumb in her mouth and worked away at her security blanket, a small square of fabric with a satin border that she inched her fingers around the perimeter of as if doing a circuit on a set of worry beads.

"But she's at her daddy's house," Pickle said. "She shouldn't be sad there."

I paused and remembered eavesdropping one afternoon on a group of twenty-something women. One of them was telling a story about how she had been living abroad and became sick. She called her father and he said he would be on the next plane if she needed him. The other girls nodded as she spoke; their fathers would have done the same thing. The scene put words and faces to a feeling I was only just then beginning to understand. At the time, Pickle was still young enough to be in a crib, but I already knew I would do anything and travel anywhere to keep her safe.

But it occurred to me while listening to the somber story of "Racing in the Streets" on that last drive to preschool that Springsteen was right: down the road, if Pickle ended up on the porch of her daddy's house, she, too, would be sad. I knew I had a few years before she looked to a life outside of our house, but already everything was moving by so fast. In the blink of an eye, the milestone of preschool was about to be behind us.

We turned into the preschool parking lot and Pickle climbed into the front seat with me to listen to the rest of the song. Ordinarily, we had time on the drive to listen to a few songs, but on that day we just kept playing "Racing in the Streets" over and over. Pickle sat on my lap for one last listen and we turned up the volume. A few moms and dads who had already dropped off their kids waved at us as they walked back to their cars. But Pickle and I were much too far away to respond. We weren't sitting on any damn porch being sad, not the two of us. We were out there racing in the street with no sign of stopping.

Look out, kindergarten, I thought, *here we come.*

18.

～～

THE *VINEYARD GAZETTE* newsroom, like most news-
rooms, is a wide-open space filled with desks. The editor
has her own office, but the rest of us—the reporters, photog-
raphers, and designers—sit in one big corral-like room. An
open newsroom can be an odd thing. If everyone is on dead-
line, the only sound is the tapping of fingers on keyboards
and the occasional crunch of a salty snack. If someone walks
across the room, the person often switches to tiptoeing, as if
entering a library. Other times, the room is a crosscurrent of
conversations: interviews being conducted by phone, stories
being strategized, the squawk of the police scanner alerting
us to everything from a serious accident to a feral turkey on
the prowl.

The whole operation is located in downtown Edgartown
in a very old house with a rabbit warren of rooms that house
the advertising staff, graphics department, and accounting.
On the roof is a weather vane in the shape of a quill, which
on windy days turns with an eerie creak.

Downstairs is the press room, where the 1974 Goss Press,
a hulking beast that shakes the whole building, still spits out
the paper each Thursday. Sometimes we actually run down

and yell, "Stop the presses!" although the pressman hates this and we try to do it as little as possible.

Community journalism is dying everywhere, something I didn't think about when I took the job, but on the island it's still alive. Advertising has plummeted, but we survive. Our base of loyal subscribers is crucial. Locals are avid readers. Seasonal residents subscribe year-round, too. They want to stay connected to news of the towns in the off-season in case they need to weigh in on something. The *Vineyard Gazette* has never missed a week since the first edition ran off the old press on May 14, 1846; oddly enough, May 14 is my birthday, too.

Every week, the reporters fan out to the board meetings in each town, to the school committee meetings, and to discussions about the Steamship Authority's ferry services. We follow every thread, from the planning boards to the sewer departments. We also track the arts and the locals, and in summer we profile the captains of industry, from arts to politics to business, who arrive for rest and relaxation but usually say yes when we call and ask for an interview, often conducted on their porch or a bench downtown, in flip-flops and T-shirts.

After a few years at the Vineyard Gazette, I had worked my way from calendar entry, to associate editor, to managing editor—but at a small weekly paper, you do every task no matter your title, from editing, to writing, to throwing out the trash.

Covering the community from cradle to grave means publishing the scope of a life: birth notices, to high school graduation, to engagements, to weddings, to obituaries. Most obituaries come from the families or funeral homes but occasionally, when someone of note dies, we write our own obituaries for them. Before I worked at the *Gazette*, I had never written an obituary. They're difficult, to say the least, but it's also an honor to give voice to a life. The lifting up of an Islander or seasonal resident, talking to a family and friends, made me feel more of a part of the community. Often, Cathlin would perform the funeral of a person whose life I had just chronicled, and this pairing of our skills made our own roots here stronger.

At some point, however, writing obituaries on a small island can't help but become extremely personal, when a few degrees of separation becomes a dear friend.

I FIRST MET the filmmaker Wes Craven when he stopped by the newspaper office one summer afternoon. He was visiting his stepdaughter, who was a summer intern at the time. I had seen many of his films, such as *Nightmare on Elm Street* and *Scream*, and expected, well, I don't know what I expected but definitely not a mild-mannered professor type who looked more like a man about to lecture on film theory than someone who had frightened moviegoers for decades. He had a close-cropped beard, and mostly hung about in the background while his wife, Iya, and I spoke. I didn't talk to Wes that day beyond saying hello and shaking his hand.

About a month later, Cathlin and I were invited to an end-of-summer cookout thrown by Iya. Again, Wes stood quietly off to the side. Someone asked me about an essay I had published that week, about me getting kidnapped while hitchhiking on the Vineyard as a young boy. Wes, who was eavesdropping, hadn't read the piece but asked a few questions about it. The next day I received an email from him. He had read my essay.

"Ever think of making this into a movie?" he asked.

"I am now," I wrote back.

We met for coffee and discussed my essay. Then we kept meeting long after we decided we couldn't figure out a way to expand it into a movie. We kept meeting because we liked each other and liked talking about writing and creativity. We met for beers and hamburgers every few months, whenever he returned to the island from Los Angeles. Eventually, Wes and Iya offered to babysit Pickle and Hardy at their house any time we needed a night off. We told Wes he could watch the kids on one condition: he wasn't allowed to show them any of his movies.

When we arrived at their home for the first babysitting night, Wes was wearing furry slippers with claws on the end. Pickle said he looked like an overgrown hobbit and the two of them quickly disappeared into the living room to talk about quests and good versus evil.

On the way to dinner, Cathlin and I texted almost everyone we knew that Wes Craven was babysitting our children.

We shared many holidays and conversations over the next few years. Wes and Iya were at our house the week before Cathlin started her chemotherapy treatments, and we all raised a glass and said a prayer as she set out on her voyage. Three years later, during a New Year's Eve party, Wes told Cathlin he had been having moments of dizziness and forgetfulness. A few weeks later he went to the hospital and was diagnosed with aggressive brain cancer.

After one of his operations, Wes sent me a photo. The subject of the email read "Open Mind." The photo was of his brain, his skull open during the operation. It was classic Wes Craven, a quiet man whose heart was always looking for humor in the darkness.

Wes died a few months after his first operation. Cathlin

performed his funeral service in Los Angeles. In the audience were many of the actors from *Scream*, crying hard, along with the scary guy from *The Hills Have Eyes*.

Back home, I wrote his obituary for the *Gazette*.

I OFTEN VISIT Wes's grave to check in with him. It's not far from my house, marked by a big unruly stone that appears plucked from an ancient stone wall.

The grave sits under a holly tree and is well tended by family, encircled with flowers and small pots with tiny peppers. Rocks of various shapes, but mostly hearts, are there, too, as are numerous Ukrainian flags; Iya is of Ukrainian descent. But my favorite are the words carved in his stone: I'LL BE RIGHT BACK. There's also a small rock resting atop the stone: WE'LL BE RIGHT BACK.

When visiting friends in a graveyard I grow quiet. I stand or sit or walk in a bit of a circle, listening to old conversations in my head, memories enjoyed over dinner or a beer or at a café. I listen to the wind and the birds and the swaying of trees—another form of quiet that says so much. And I listen to the current conversation we're having because it's ongoing, and oddly enough doesn't feel one sided, even when looking at dates with a beginning and an end.

Once, when Wes and I were talking about writing and creativity, he likened the process to a cat. "If you stare at it, it won't come," he said. "Look away; not long after you'll feel its fur brush up against you. Once it touches you, you can touch it."

"Yes, that's it," I replied at the time, and again while visiting his grave. *That's exactly it.*

19.

WHEN PICKLE MOVED up to kindergarten, she began attending the school close to our house where Hardy went, a public charter school near enough that we could bike or even walk to it through a path in the woods. Pickle was an early walker and an early talker. She took to bike riding early, too, and soon the three of us were setting off each morning, helmets and backpacks in place. I anchored our lineup, so on the ride I couldn't see Pickle's face and had to imagine whether she was smiling or in deep concentration as she tried to keep up with her brother. I marveled at this small creature in front of me.

At first we all rode together, but as the months and then years passed, Hardy began to surge ahead and we met him at the school parking lot. Then, for a time, we would all enter the school holding hands.

I can still remember the day I reached for Hardy's hand and he rejected it, choosing instead to acknowledge my presence with only a brief nod. It was his first day of fifth grade. He was ten years old.

Pickle was starting first grade that year, a big jump from kindergarten, a whole new world, it felt to me at the time.

She told me the night before her first day that she was both nervous and excited. "That's the perfect way to feel about a new adventure," I said.

The next day, walking through the hallways, I saw the familiar faces of teachers and students, and parents, too, most of whom I had known since Hardy started kindergarten. Some parents were smiling, some tried to hide their tears, the beginning of another school year always an emotional moment. As we talked and updated one another on our summers, we also shared our sadness, right there next to the pencil sharpeners and jars of paste, that our little ones were growing up so quickly. Later, after the morning orientation meeting had ended and I shuffled out of the school, I looked around at all the parents in the schoolyard.

Before you become a parent you have no idea that this other first-day-of-school scene exists: some adults run to their cars, happy to have a few hours to themselves, while others mill about the parking lot unsure of what to do next.

It reminded me of something my dad said to me just before Hardy was born. He said, "You have no idea what's about to hit you." At the time, I didn't like his comment. It seemed to have a bit of comeuppance to it, a "Now you'll see how hard it is" tone. But after Hardy was born, I realized my father's comment was the most accurate truism another parent had shared with me. The enormity of the highs and the lows of parenting can't be explained nor prepared for. Parenting defined my every waking minute, and if I ever forgot this, my children were sure to remind me, usually in the dark of night when they cried out from their beds that they were scared or thirsty or couldn't find their favorite stuffed animal.

The schoolyard scene also took me back to a time when I was just starting out as a father, a time when I felt completely adrift.

FOR THE FIRST five years of Hardy's life, I was a stay-at-home dad. It was an uneasy fit. We were living in New York City, and instead of going to work each day, I suddenly found myself wandering the streets pushing my son on Herculean stroller walks until my Achilles tendon finally gave out. We switched to loitering in cafés. Over many cappuccinos and sippy cups of warmed breast milk, I taught Hardy baby sign language until we could converse like a couple of third-base coaches. I took him to wrestling matches and swim meets at Columbia University, near our apartment. At night, after Hardy and Cathlin fell asleep, I watched episodes of *The Wire* and felt as though the characters in the show were my only friends.

At first it didn't occur to me, because my son wasn't even a toddler yet, to go to the playground. But one day I wandered by and was amazed to see so many parents and kids there. I was both excited and nervous standing on the perimeter of the park, like a freshman quaking at the sight of the high school lunchroom.

I noticed a few other stay-at-home dads, but I didn't want to approach them. I figured any other stay-at-home dads were losers. The irony wasn't lost on me, but the truth is that anyone looking out on a playground knows that the moms are the stars of the show—they're the major leaguers, the Oscar winners, the cool kids who not only know how to take care of their babies but had also gestated and birthed them and fed them with their own bodies. Compared to that, a man is a janitor able to clean up a mess and not much more.

But the moms also seemed too rarefied to approach.

Thankfully, a group of Jamaican nannies took me in. I was overjoyed to finally be part of a group. We would meet up each day at the park, and I would hear tales of their lives growing up in Jamaica and also about how after taking care of someone else's child all day, they would go home to care for their own sons and daughters. I wish I could do those women justice here on the page, as they were so important to me—but how can I when I see now that I didn't do them justice in real life, either. The moment a mom showed an interest in me, I moved on.

It happened unexpectedly.

I was pushing Hardy in a baby swing when a mom came over and began pushing her son next to me. She was incredible, playing with her son's toes, doing underdogs, even lying down on the ground beneath the swing to make her boy laugh. It was from this position that she looked up at me and said, "Hi. What's your boy's name? Mine's is Elijah."

Her name was Jessica. She was a mixture of a New York City tough and an Ivory Soap girl. She had short black hair, pale skin, and a tattoo of a dove on her shoulder. After I'd introduced her to Cathlin, she said, "Oh, wow, she's beautiful."

"Oh, really," I said, smiling. "I never noticed."

Cathlin punched me in the arm, but she was smiling, too.

Jessica introduced me to a whole group of moms—Paula, Jee Yoon, Jen, Deb, and Nim—and I quickly became a part of their club. That was the moment I realized how fast fellow parents can bond and become an essential part of each other's lives. My friendships before parenthood were gradual journeys, picking up tidbits like scattered crumbs and only over months or years forming a tight bond. But with parenting, everything is laid bare and so much is shared so quickly that within an hour or two it's as if you'd never not known this other parent you just met. We were also in a sense the walking wounded: sleep deprived, often unwashed, and wrestling with lives that had been changed by the sudden appearance of our child. We were like a series of rafts lashed together to ride out a storm.

Around the time our firstborns turned four years old and our second kids arrived, we all moved out of New York City as quickly and as choreographed as if a curtain had come down to announce the end of the first act. We moved to Massachusetts, Washington, and California, to the New York suburbs and to Martha's Vineyard. We quickly immersed ourselves in new groups of parents, the relationships once again forged faster than I'd have believed possible, and the memories of those who had been so close were lost in the everyday scrum of parenting.

WHEN I PICKED up Pickle and Hardy at the end of that first day of school, I was still thinking about those old days in New York and the children of my mom friends. I had no idea what they even looked like now, those kids who for a time I'd have defended with my life.

I watched Hardy come out the school's front door and noticed from a distance how his thick hair cascaded down to his back, how his shoulders were growing broader. *How long until his voice changes?* I wondered.

I was so distracted by the thought that when Hardy reached out to take my hand, he surprised me. It had been so long since he had done this that the size of his hand startled me. Before I could stop myself, I jerked my hand away from his. By the time I realized what I'd done, Hardy had already moved past me, striding toward his bike, unaware that his father was nearly knocked to his knees by the wave of emotion washing over him. My father was right: once again, I had no idea what had hit me.

20.

ONCE A WEEK for years, I stopped at Lynn Irons's house on my way to work. Her driveway was usually blocked by a dump truck and assorted wheelbarrows. To the left side, a tilting chicken coop, home to a dozen or so hens, was being slowly overtaken by bamboo.

Lynn is the *Vineyard Gazette*'s garden columnist. She doesn't like computers, so she writes the column by hand. For years, it was my job to stop by her house each week to pick up her column, which usually waited for me under a rock outside her side door. Lynn moved to the Vineyard in the 1960s, having grown up Appalachian-poor in western Pennsylvania, something she often refers to in her column, tucked in among her advice on growing vegetables. She ends each column with a liberal stance against whatever injustice has taken place in the world that week. Sometimes it is an abrupt turn: one moment she is in her garden or canning shed taking in the harvest and the next she is calling out a national political figure for his many misdeeds.

One day, when I stopped for my weekly pickup, there was no column awaiting me beneath the rock by Lynn's door. I knocked and let myself in with a "Hello?" Lynn was seated at her kitchen table.

"Bill," she said. There had been a heavy morning dew, she explained, so her column was on the kitchen counter, where it would stay dry. I spotted it beside some bills and books about the downfall of our country.

"I did the dumbest thing," Lynn said. "I took in two kittens."

I looked down at the big cage next to her kitchen table. One extremely white kitten sat in it licking his paws.

"I only see one."

"I know. I've already lost the other one. I think she's in the piano."

We both grew quiet, slowed our breath, and concentrated but heard nothing.

Lynn's canning equipment was spread across the kitchen table, along with dozens of tomatoes and some dilly beans. She was getting ready for winter, making sure nothing from her garden went to waste. When I tutored Lynn's granddaughter for her SATs, I refused to take any money, so Lynn paid me in food—dilly beans, tomato sauce, a ham after she butchered her pig. I also took advice about topics such as when to put the winter rye down in my small garden and how to grow asparagus, a three-year commitment before even a nub reveals itself.

"Damn, I have to get to work," Lynn said. "But if I don't find the kitten before I leave, I don't know if she'll survive."

Together, we moved the piano in the living room and checked the inner workings, but found nothing. I had never been deeper into Lynn's house than the kitchen. Passing the pantry, I saw shelves filled with canned food and mason jars of water. Lynn noticed me looking and said, "In case Armageddon comes . . . which is actually already here."

We searched a few more places but couldn't find the second kitten, and I had to leave for work. Lynn's column was the last piece of the puzzle for getting our Nature section ready to print.

Later in the day I called to check on the kitten. Although Lynn didn't use email, she carried a cellphone with her in the fields. My call went to her voicemail. She was often out of range for cell service, a normal occurrence on the island, and could only text: "Kitten found. All good. And don't mess up the spelling of *astilbe*."

21.

⁓

AT SOME POINT, our kids began to enjoy hearing stories of their parents' past lives. On the surface we were Mom and Dad, the people they saw every day who were at their beck and call to cater to their every whim; at least that's what it sometimes felt like. But there came a time when Hardy and Pickle wanted to peel back the present to learn a bit about who we had been before they arrived, or further back even, to the time before Cathlin and I were married. The stranger the story, the more they liked it.

One of their favorites was about the man who lived in my car.

WHEN I MOVED to New York City, in the late 1980s, I brought my junker of a car with me. Being from the New Jersey suburbs, my car felt essential and it wasn't something I was ready to give up.

I was ill prepared for the city. I had just graduated from college and my existence to that point had been one of leafy expanses and fresh air. New York felt like a punch in the face, the pace, the noise, the urban gray. Once I'd soaked it all up,

I decided it was perfect. Except for the parking. While a garage cost almost as much as my rent, finding a spot on the street was a full-time job. I was living in Tribeca, which back then was still considered living on the edge. The warehouses had not yet been converted to luxury condos. Bazzini Nuts did, in fact, sell nuts and not lattes. The only signs of night life were restaurants, such as Odeon and Bouley. Yet it still took hours to find a parking spot.

One day, while walking to the subway, I noticed that the street around Duane Park was free of NO PARKING signs. At the time, Duane Park was a park in name only. Mostly, it was a circle of macadam with a few benches. It was also a gathering spot for homeless people.

I asked around about the lack of signs. A cabbie told me a story about how one moonless night some guy, fed up with too many parking tickets, had hacked down all the signs. Why they hadn't returned, the cabbie couldn't say. Whether or not the story was true, I never investigated. I didn't care—I just wanted one of those spots. And so on a gorgeous Labor Day weekend, when everyone else was at the beach, I hung back, lying in wait.

My reward, the best parking spot in the city, turned out to be a mixed blessing. Whenever I thought about using my car, I worried about someone taking my spot. There was only one solution: I stopped driving altogether. To avoid temptation, I avoided my car, walking the long way home from the subway each day. I did this for months. As a result, I didn't know that a man had moved into my car.

I discovered him Thanksgiving morning, or, rather, we discovered him. Cathlin and I had been dating for two months. From the initial ask at the funeral back home in

New Jersey to our first date at a dive bar called the Holiday Cocktail Lounge, in the East Village, we were slowly getting to know each other again. We had a shared past but not a present, not yet at least. While I tried to understand her life as a seminarian, she was curious about me, a young man who hadn't yet found his way.

I had moved to New York to work at a bank. I didn't like my job, but thought it was something I was supposed to do—in fact, most of my life back then consisted of doing things that seemed guaranteed to change me as little as possible. New York, a place where so many move to reinvent themselves, became for me simply a grittier version of life as I had always known it. When I wasn't working, I behaved like a cliché twenty-something living in the Big Apple for the first time: I hung out at bars and drank too much with former classmates and coworkers.

Secretly, I thought the only reason Cathlin had been interested in me was because she still saw me as an upperclassman from high school, someone she once looked up to just because I was older. But there we were, officially dating and about to drive home on Thanksgiving, to travel together and share the holiday with our families—it was a big step up from my late-night journeys to her basement in the old days. For the occasion, I decided it was time to drive my car again.

It was a cold morning, and as we walked to my car, I could hear our footsteps crunching on the first frost of the season. Up ahead, I noticed a small, flickering light coming from inside my car. We approached the back window, looked in, and saw a homeless man curled up beside a few tea candles. He looked cozy back there, covered in a blanket and surrounded by bags of clothing and a plate of rice and beans.

I looked around, half expecting a camera crew to pop out and shout *Surprise*!, the setup to a practical joke. But the street was deserted. A frigid wind blew off the Hudson River.

There was no way I could roust a homeless man on Thanksgiving morning.

"I guess we'll have to take the train home," I said to Cathlin.

Some may have looked at that moment and decided I wasn't the guy for them, but Cathlin smiled, reached out her hand, and we took a new step in our life together, our fingers intertwined as we headed to the subway station while in my car a homeless man slept soundly.

What followed was a friendship of sorts with the man in my car, or that's what I told myself. He continued to live in my car and I continued to give him space, while also spying on him from time to time. I casually walked by on the way to work, checking to see if he was home but never stopping to introduce myself. Late at night, after last call, my friends and I would walk down to Duane Street. If the man was home, I made sure everyone kept out of sight, but if he was out, we approached the car and peered into his life. His belongings began to take up more room in the car. The backseat overflowed with bags and food cartons.

I was still struck that I let the man stay in my car, but I never stopped to say hello. It wasn't that I was afraid of him. Instead, I wanted him to stay, and I was worried that if I tried to talk to him, he'd get spooked and move. He had become a part of my life, something unique that I thought set me apart from the average crowd milling around at the bar. Instead of starting every conversation with a reference to college or my nightmare boss, I began to open with "So, there's this guy living in my car . . ."

But more important, it was an experience and a charged period of my life I was sharing with Cathlin: the mystery of who the man was and the mystery of who I was becoming.

Eventually, I stopped bringing friends by the car; it didn't feel right, an invasion of the man's space that risked making him a spectacle or oddity on display. But Cathlin and I still walked down to Duane Street at night, taking note of the incongruity of the limousines parked and waiting for fares as they dined at Bouley, while next to them sat my VW Golf, now more apartment than automobile.

Occasionally, the man would disappear and stay away for several days. Whenever this happened, I feared the worst, that he had found some new place to stay or had succumbed in some way to the harsh realities of being without a home. But eventually he returned, and the sight of him made me so happy that I wanted to shake his hand and ask how his trip had been. But I continued to say nothing, even when he started decorating.

It began discreetly enough, around the holidays, with some figures etched into the grime of the windshield. A snowman, then a Santa, and finally a herd of reindeer on the side windows. Soon, a small Christmas tree appeared off the right front bumper. A large wreath was hung from the front grille. My car began to look like a present too big to be put under the tree, so it had been left in the street.

The end arrived later that winter, when I received a call from the police. The officer I spoke with was shocked to learn I already knew that a man was living in my car.

"You just let him stay?" he asked incredulously.

"I found him Thanksgiving morning," I said. "It felt like the right thing to do."

"The right thing to do would have been to call the cops," he replied.

The officer had kicked the guy out of my car. When I asked if he knew anything about the man, the officer paused.

"No," he said. "Nothing out of the ordinary. Just a homeless guy. We told him he had to leave and he walked away toward the river."

Later that afternoon I walked to my car, opened the door, and, for the first time in months, sat in the driver's seat. There were piles of clothes everywhere, along with newspapers and food wrappers.

I rolled down the window, stuck my key in the ignition, and turned it. Silence. The battery had died long ago. I went to a payphone and called a tow truck, and then made another call, to Cathlin. She arrived soon after and we both sat in my car and waited. I felt sad and we didn't talk much. But when I picture the two of us just starting out together, seated in the front seat of a car that wasn't going anywhere, I can't help but smile.

THE NIGHT I first told this story at the dinner table, Hardy and Pickle shook their heads and rolled their eyes. "You should've talked to the man," they said. Then they asked what happened to the car.

"It was an old car and not worth anything, so I gave it to the tow truck guy in exchange for him taking it away," I said. "That part of my life was over."

The kids nodded, then asked a few more questions to verify the story. Then they headed off to watch TV while Cathlin and I sat at the table, raising our glasses to toast the people we once were.

22.

~~

A FEW TIMES A year, I go to the Martha's Vineyard Regional High School to teach a writing class. I usually work with the juniors, focusing on the personal essay as they begin to think about their college application essays.

I start each class with an introduction, talking about my experiences from high school to the present. I tell them I had always been a reader and wanted to write more when I was their age but was afraid and so completed only what was assigned in class. I tell them how on my first day of college all freshmen had to write an essay to gauge what class they were ready for. An excellent essay exempted a student from taking any English class; a terrible essay warranted a remedial writing class. I tell them I was sent to the bottom.

The experience of being judged inferior on the first day of college had a lasting impact. I did well in the remedial writing class and actually enjoyed it but couldn't get over the feeling that I would forever be a bad writer. I avoided all literature and writing classes after that and turned to economics, a subject that didn't interest me but felt safe. After college I became a banker, though I mostly focused on drinking and getting to know New York City, where I had moved.

A few years later, I saved myself by applying to a program called Princeton in Asia and moved away to teach English in northern Thailand. I had finally succeeded in displacing myself, leaving everything and everyone I knew in order to make sense of who I was and what I actually wanted to do. I needed to do something extreme, I tell the high school students, in order to become a blank slate.

In Thailand, I began reading again and writing letters, taking baby steps but ones that gave me such pleasure that I knew I was on my way somewhere. When I returned home to New York City, I began taking classes at night at the Writers Studio and continued doing so for ten years, after work and on weekends, eventually becoming a teacher there as well as a student. Later, at the age of thirty-eight, I went to graduate school and studied writing full time.

I don't tell my story to the students to convince them to embark on a writing career because often I feel it's too much work with little to show for it—I joke that it's a disease, and yet it's also the thing that made me the person I always wanted to be. I tell the students about my journey to plant the seed that it's okay to search and that at some point, if they keep their eyes, ears, and heart open, they may catch a glimpse of what they're actually called to do rather than what they think they should do.

At the end of each class, after we've read our essay attempts out loud, I tell the students that if anyone wants help with their college essays, they can reach out to me. I have only one rule: I don't charge for this. Every fall, about fifteen students take me up on the offer. For a few busy Saturdays and Sundays, they wander in and out of my house, carrying their computers or pens and paper, along with stories of who they are and who they want to become. My main advice is for them to write about something they care about, not what they think a college counselor wants to hear, and to write in their own voice. But often it's not easy recognizing what you care about, and so we scrape away at the surface looking for nuggets of feeling, from a young man who tells me about staying up all night in a barn during lambing season to help with the birthing process to a young woman who wants to reconnect with her five-year-old self, when she wasn't afraid to be curious and to be herself. It's my own version of the Writers Studio, re-creating a time and place that changed me forever, right there at the kitchen table or, if the weather is nice, on the front porch.

The essay work is always so open and honest that after a student leaves I find myself thinking about the story of my own life for a moment. Then I get back to work, trying to tell it and live it the best I can.

23.

～～

During Cathlin's cancer treatments, I had posted some essays I wrote about the experience on Facebook. Friends old and new sent notes of support and helped me feel less alone. Not only had the island community been with us, but names and faces from my past had been beside me, too.

A former professor of mine from graduate school, Ned Stuckey-French, responded not only with his heart but also with his mind, checking in about both Cathlin's health and my writing about the experience. At graduate school, Ned taught nonfiction writing and the personal essay. His class gave me my first taste of the genre.

Even though Ned wasn't much older than I was when we first met, I was a student and he was a professor, so there was a divide. But reconnecting years later seemed to put us on equal ground. We were friends, navigating family and work and writing the best we could, and sharing the experience.

Then one day Ned sent a note saying he had cancer. It was early still and the details unclear, he said. But when the details did surface, they weren't good. When Ned died, not long after his diagnosis, I traveled back to Tallahassee for the services.

I HAD BECOME Ned's student when, at the age of thirty-eight, I entered the graduate writing program at Florida State University, in Tallahassee, to finally embrace without restraint what had been in my heart since childhood, but had always been afraid to face. To be a writer and to be a father are the only two things I've always known I wanted—oddly enough, I became both in Tallahassee, a place so foreign to my northeastern roots that the Spanish moss dripping off the live oaks seemed more like a movie set detail than a happenstance of nature. Cathlin and I had been married for two years when we moved to Florida. She not only said yes to this turn of events, including my saying no to the safety and structure of a high-paying job; she also gave me the strength to say yes to confusion, worry, and a life if not well lived, then at least lived as it was meant for me.

When classes began, Ned asked all of us why we were there: *Why write? Why set out on this grueling obsession?* I went first, the words churning in my head, desperate to be spoken out loud. I said I never felt completely myself until I found writing, the simple act of watching words appear from beneath the point of my pencil. "I write," I said, "because it's like breathing . . . I simply have no choice if I want to be whole."

To Ned's credit, he didn't pause or panic at this outpouring, or let the words fall too heavily on this class of mostly twenty-somethings.

"Bill just testified," he said. "He showed himself. Who's next?"

Someone else spoke up, then someone else. But I have no recollection of what anyone else said. I had startled myself by being so vulnerably honest among a group of strangers.

AT NED'S MEMORIAL service I saw his wife Elizabeth, who was also one of my professors, his children, and my former professors. I listened to everyone tell beautiful stories about Ned, but I didn't linger after the service. Instead, I felt the urge to walk, drive, and bike into my past. I ate food I had once eaten regularly, eavesdropped on accents I had adored, and spent time at Harden's Taxidermy, in the southern Georgia town of Thomasville, just an hour north of Tallahassee.

I first encountered Harden's when Cathlin and I dropped off our U-Haul rental after moving from New York City. The shop catered to local hunters but alongside boar, deer, and snakes, there were Arctic foxes from Alaskan hunting trips, and a huge rhinoceros head from an African safari featured prominently. For Ned's class, my first attempt at nonfiction, I decided to spend a week at Harden's, watching, listening, and writing about the place and the people who worked there. After class ended each afternoon, I drove up to Harden's and hung out until closing time. When I revisited Harden's years later, the place seemed smaller and Ed, the owner, was not around to reminisce with. The smell of glue still overpowered me, and the animals, trapped in time on the walls or mounted on stands on the floor, looked exactly the same. I patted a few snouts, rubbed the bristly hair of a boar, and touched the teeth of a coiled rattlesnake.

When I finished the first draft of the Harden's essay and delivered it to Ned, he suggested I delete the whole first page.

"It starts at page two," he said.

That wasn't all he said—there was praise, too—but, really, that was all he needed to say. He had nailed it.

I also wrote an essay in class about Cathlin working as a hospice chaplain, driving down the back roads and administering spiritual care, sometimes in dirt-floor shacks. She was pregnant at the time and when the baby began to show, her patients called her "the little pregnant preacher."

Ned's specialty was the essay in all its forms. He liked to say that it was a journey of the mind, filled with the contradictions of being both personal and public—it had to have form and structure but could also be open to meandering, much like life itself.

He also introduced me to the essays of Edward Hoagland, who years later I would discover lived a few blocks from the *Vineyard Gazette*. When I convinced Hoagland to write pieces for the *Gazette* and sent them to Ned, my old teacher could barely contain his joy at this weaving together in our lives' narratives.

MY RETURN TO Harden's Taxidermy and wandering around Tallahassee's fringes was interrupted by a text from Cathlin. She was checking to see how I was doing, and also told me about at an event at her church celebrating the work of the eco-theologian Thomas Berry. The authors of Berry's biography had come to give a talk. Reading Cathlin's text from the present while I was in Florida exploring my past brought me back to my time with the nuns at Genesis Farm. They followed the teachings of Berry, who preached a return-to-the-earth gospel; he called himself a "geologian."

When I went on my retreat to Genesis Farm, I was trying to make sense of many things, but a few in particular: my still hidden desire to write, my advancing age, and how my wife's call to the ministry fit into my life. Through fasting and silence, the retreat was designed to help guide people at a crossroads in their lives. Although there were other seekers, it was basically one long slog with the self. A lack of distractions and ordinary rhythms, I discovered, can bring a man to his knees.

To pass the time out in the woods, I began building creatures out of twigs and leaves and stones on the forest floor, then inventing their storylines. The creations grew larger as I switched from sticks to logs, from stones to boulders. On the last day, I spent a long time on what would become a giant woman, perhaps an inner compulsion to put form to Mother Earth, I thought while building it. But when I had finished and began to tell myself the story of this woman, I discovered I had created an image of my wife, one that was overcome with sadness.

Alone in the woods, I realized that since our wedding, just a few months earlier, Cathlin and I had grown apart. It was gradual, a day-to-day deepening of unease that I didn't understand. We had known each other since we were teenagers, had lived together for the past two years, and only now, after an actual wedding, did our relationship feel off. I didn't think marriage would change a thing—but that was my problem, I realized. I was still living as if nothing had changed. I had not given myself over to marriage.

I spent that night throwing up, physically overcome by the emotions that had surfaced while I was alone in the woods.

The next day, I drove home, sat with Cathlin on the couch, and told her what I had experienced. And although October 6 is the date of our anniversary, the day my parents call and our children make us cards, our real wedding took place on that day, just the two of us holding each other and weeping on the couch.

Not long after, we moved to Tallahassee.

AFTER MY TEXT conversation with Cathlin, I sat back on my bunk. I was staying at a youth hostel in Tallahassee. There were two sets of bunk beds and new roommates came and went. All the hotels had been booked because there was a home football game, and at FSU that changes the whole city as fans flock to Tallahassee.

The hostel was a long way from a retreat with nuns in New Jersey, but the proximity and anonymity of my roommates, along with the spartan furnishings, did feel familiar. So did the depth of my reflections.

How do you process and add up the enormity of a life? I wondered. How to give each small piece its due so that a path, no matter how circuitous, becomes visible in hindsight. I had chosen, as if by coincidence, to work with the nuns, and then by gut to attend their retreat. I had chosen to attend FSU in much the same way. When Cathlin and I moved to Martha's Vineyard to take care of my grandmother, I knew I needed something at that moment in my life, but wasn't exactly sure where and how it would reveal itself. Ned and his class, along with other professors and classes, gave me the tools to both excavate the past and feel more comfortable in the present, knowing that if I was at least paying close attention to my life, I was in some way moving in the right direction, even if I couldn't see the signs.

But the throughline, I understood while sitting on that hostel bunk bed, was Cathlin. She had always believed that the future would take care of itself if in the present you followed your heart.

Not giving over to her, not giving over to writing, not giving over to fatherhood, not giving over to spirituality and religion as she practiced it, all were examples of not so much fear but a lack of faith. The wilderness is uncomfortable and there's no getting around it—nor should there be.

I wished I could have told Ned all this when we reconnected years after we met as teacher and student, but I've also come to believe that the ghosts of our past continue to walk with us. And so by writing this down, feeling it again on the page, I was continuing the conversation.

AT THE END of Ned's memorial service, I said hello to Elizabeth. She was surprised to see me. I hadn't told her I was making the trip, and perhaps she didn't know that Ned and I had kept in touch via emails and our shared love of Edward Hoagland's essays. But then again, who among us really knows the effect we have on others, the ones we live with, see every day, or especially those we spend only a small portion of our lives with.

That's another reason why I traveled back to Tallahassee: to let her know by my presence what Ned had done for me: He had helped me to *testify.*

24.

~~~

I WAS AT THE *Gazette* office, editing a piece about nitrogen issues in the local ponds, when I received an email from a high school friend who still lived in New Jersey, not far from our hometown. Tommy usually caught me up on local gossip. We were on the wrestling team together and he kept track of what teams looked good and told me which wrestlers to keep an eye on.

But this note carried with it harder news. Tommy had emailed me an article about a young man who had recently died of a drug overdose. He was a former wrestler, a great one who had been a New Jersey state champ and then went to an Ivy League college. He was also the son of one of my high school wrestling adversaries. Chris became my main competitor when he appeared out of nowhere my senior year. He was a stud from western Jersey who moved to the town next to mine and quickly proceeded to give me my first regular-season loss in three years.

After I read the article, I left the office and went for a walk. I didn't want to let myself imagine too much. Beyond the story of the death, I knew nothing about Chris's son except for a few newspaper clippings about his wrestling career. Mostly, I thought of Chris on that walk, a fellow father whose grief I couldn't fathom. I had not seen or spoken to Chris in more than three decades. I had no idea what he even looked like now, so I thought of him as he was, with thick red hair and dressed in his wrestling warmups, trying to break a sweat before one of our matches.

Wrestling becomes an obsession for anyone hooked by the sport, a way of contracting the world to the simplicity of a mano-a-mano existence. There are no teammates to worry about or coach's decisions to complain about. On the mat, when the whistle blows, everything else disappears.

The training is physically demanding, too, which is another reason it appealed to me, and I imagine to Chris, also. Every night after practice, I ran through the streets, from one end of town to the other. As the season deepened and the leaves fell, the crunch of almost every footstep seemed to echo outward as if to say, "Watch out, this kid means business!" Some nights I ran with bricks in my hands, a training technique I used to build up my wind and my arms at the same time. Your biceps stay tight the entire run and soon your arms are more like lead weights than useful appendages; to lift them at all is nearly impossible.

Occasionally, even after carrying the bricks and finishing my workout with wind sprints, I still wasn't tired enough. My heart felt so huge that I turned around and started the run again, from Belmont Avenue to Mountain Avenue, then parallel along Route 22, where cars were headed east, perhaps to New York City, my future home, but not even in my imagination yet. My world then was confined to New Jersey towns, those nearby and a few farther away, where opponents lurked. I knew those kids by name from the newspaper, wrestling camps, and summer tournaments: *Melchiore, Jacoutot, Monize, Kelly.* I can still see the faces of those boys—they're men now, but always seventeen in my mind, lean and strong and waiting for me.

Over the years, I had thought about Chris, this boy who once occupied my every waking moment for a full year of my life and then I never saw again. The images of those days come back without warning or fanfare, perhaps on a run, or while I'm driving and a certain song comes on the radio, or when I wrestle with my kids in the living room or backyard. My heart will quicken and no matter what I'm doing, I'm suddenly a teenager again, running through the streets of my hometown late at night, feeling so strong and free that it's as if I might lift off and fly.

As I traveled back to a time when our problems seemed to rarely extend beyond the wrestling mat, the memory felt like a balm. But the longer I walked, the less I thought about our glory days, and the more I thought about a grieving father.

WHEN I ARRIVED home that night, all I wanted to do was to hug my children and tell them how much I loved them. Instead, I ended up in an argument with Hardy over something small that escalated out of control until we were both yelling and he ran to his room in tears.

I went to sleep early that night, feeling so confused and awful about fighting with Hardy that I wanted to disappear. In bed, the reason for our argument began to dawn on me: it happened because I was scared. We carry the weight of protecting our children like we carry the blood in our veins: it's ever present. We hope we've done enough to protect them, but also know that a lot is out of our control.

The next day, I wondered how to tell Hardy that every time I looked at him I was overcome with love and worry, that I moved both back in time to when he was a baby and forward to when he'll be a man. Parenting in the present can be such a crowded place, with memories of the past and fears of the future blocking the way.

I knocked on Hardy's door, walked into his room, and sat down on his bed. I began by apologizing and then tried to explain that fathers are human, too, and that I was upset and sad over something that had nothing to do with him. He shrugged and nodded and told me I had been kind of frightening the night before. Then he made a joke and began walking toward his door as if to say, "Okay, Dad, good talk . . . we're done now."

But I wasn't ready to let him go.

"Hey," I said. "Want to wrestle?"

We began doing some moves, arm drags and duck-unders, fireman's carries and single leg take-downs, laughing and having fun. Hardy thought we were just wrestling, but with every move I was hugging him and holding on to him— and, although I knew it was impossible, wishing I would never have to let him go.

25.

WHEN I BECAME a parent, my gaze felt firmly planted in the present. I watched for my children's first glimmers of recognition, a sign that they knew me, their father. I watched for their first smile, their first laugh. I watched them roll over, sit up, find their fingers and toes. I watched them pull themselves up at a low table and slowly walk its perimeter. I watched their first unsteady steps, falling over and over again. I watched them clutch a Cheerio in their chubby fingers. I watched them cry and I watched them sleep. I watched them watch me.

Then at some point, my gaze widened.

Sometimes my mind moved ahead, wondering what kind of people my children would become or what I might do to help them succeed.

Just as often, though, my mind visited the past. As Hardy and Pickle grew into their own selves, developed their personalities and peculiarities, I kept reliving my own life as a young boy. I saw the things I once loved to do and wanted to share with them, and I saw the many mistakes I made along the way.

26.

———

WHEN I WAS sixteen, before I got my driver's license, I would bike seven miles each day after school to a gym to work out. The gym had Nautilus equipment, which was relatively new at the time, so I felt that the long bike ride was worth it.

The ride took me uphill, out of my small town nestled in the floodplains of the Watchung Mountains and into the wealthier mountain towns where the roads were lined with the mansions and views, and no one worried about what heavy rainstorms could do to their cellar.

After my workout, I biked home downhill, rarely touching the brakes. One afternoon, a woman in a station wagon didn't see me coasting along and made a sharp left turn in front of me. I can still recall every vivid detail of the accident, her front bumper, shiny and metallic, coming toward me, and I knowing that I wasn't going to clear it. The car caught my back tire and sent me tumbling down the road. When I finally stopped rolling, I saw that I was bleeding from a good-sized cut on my leg. My shoulder ached but nothing felt broken. My bike lay by the road several yards behind me, a mangled wreck.

The driver leaped from her car and raced over to check on me. Once we established that I was mostly okay physically, she offered to give me a ride home. We put my bike—now more a pile of puzzle pieces than a mode of transportation—on the backseat. We drove in silence, both still shaking and too shocked to talk. It felt like a miracle to be sitting there bleeding on her seat covers instead of headed to the hospital, or worse. I must have mumbled some directions to my house, but I have no recollection of speaking.

The woman paid for the broken bike and my medical expenses. I was only a few months from turning seventeen, so my parents suggested I use the bicycle money to start saving for a used car. But I had a better idea: I wanted to buy a used moped that a friend was selling. I had enough to buy it that week. My parents said no way.

I became incredibly angry at their decision. It was my money, I reasoned, so who were they to say no. "You have no right!" I argued, with the passion of a sixteen-year-old with no clue about life but certain of his superiority. In my defense, I think the fact that blood had been shed on my way to "earning" the money played a part in my heated response—my skin was literally in the game.

My parents stood firm. "You'll hurt yourself," they said. They never said the words *die* or *death*, at least not in my presence, but of course that's what they were afraid of. For some reason, despite the bike crash, the thought of injuring myself on the moped never crossed my mind. I thought my parents were being mean to me when they were really only loving me.

But I was sixteen and self-assured, so I retaliated—and I did it in a way that to this day makes me wonder how I could have been so cruel: I stopped talking to them for almost two months. As clear as that car's bumper catching my back tire is the image of my mother sitting at my bedside weeping, but I still didn't speak to her.

Another image comes to mind: A few weeks before the bike accident, my older brother, Jim, left for his freshman year of college. We had shared a room our entire lives. We shared friends. We spent winter afternoons together on the wrestling mat and summers on the Vineyard at each other's side. Whereas some brothers argue and beat each other up, we did neither. I loved my brother with my whole teenage heart, and when he left for college I cried myself to sleep every night for a week. When I think back to those days, I can see now that I was in a state of mourning when I was lashing out at my parents with the silent treatment.

Jim came home from college for a week around Thanksgiving and with equal parts pointed questioning ("What the hell are you doing!?") and firmness ("Get over yourself!"), he stepped in and fixed the situation. I did as he said, thankfully.

MY PARENTS AND I have never talked about those hard weeks after the bike accident, and for a long time it remained buried in the recesses of my memory. Then one weekend it resurfaced when there was a horrible moped accident on Martha's Vineyard. The young woman survived but lost a leg. I was so shaken by the news that I decided to tell Hardy and Pickle my story. They looked aghast when I described how I treated Grandma and Pawpy.

"What the hell were you thinking, dad?" Hardy asked. He sounded like my older brother.

I told him I didn't really know, even after all these years, but that there was also more to the story, something I never told my parents.

About a year after the bike accident, not long before high school graduation, I told my children, a buddy and I went for a ride on his moped. Even though I had never driven a moped, he let me drive. I felt confident as we hummed along. We'd been riding for a few miles, cruising at maybe fifteen miles an hour, when on a tight turn the front wheel locked. I sailed over the handlebars and my buddy flew off the back. We were both cut up badly but not seriously hurt. I wore long pants for weeks, even into summer, to hide the road-rash scabs from my parents.

I still have the scars and I showed them to Hardy and Pickle, particularly a thick one on my thigh. That scar means a lot to me. As a young man, it reminded me of how much my parents loved me and tried to protect me. And now that I'm a parent, it connects me to the pain of parents everywhere, trying so hard to keep their kids safe but knowing it's never enough.

27.

I WAS ONE OF three brothers. Growing up, we ate a lot of meat, compared scars, had pushup contests, and not only wrestled competitively at school but also in our basement, up and down the stairs, and in the backyard on summer nights.

Our mom was like a den mother trying to tame a pack of wolves. We knew we were an impossible handful, and so we loved her even more because she fed us, clothed us, and hardly ever broke down—at least not in front of us.

As for our father, we felt he was one of us until he fell hard for Olivia Newton-John and her sad Australian yearning wafted through the house. He had mellowed, his manhood blown away by a high-speed hair dryer. We countered with Zeppelin, the Stones, and AC/DC.

When I became a father, Taylor Swift became my Olivia Newton-John. I remember sitting with an American Girl doll in my lap and listening to Taylor sing that she was feeling twenty-two, while Pickle painted my fingernails a lovely shade of violet. Then she gave me a lip-gloss makeover and asked whether my colors were fall or summer (definitely summer).

Once, while working through a set of pushups, Pickle told me I should be more like regular daddies.

"What do you mean?" I asked on an exhale.

"Like daddies who play dolls with their daughters without doing exercises at the same time," Pickle said.

"Trust me, we're all like this," I said. "Some just hide it better than others. Now, hop on my back. I need some more weight for these pushups to feel a good muscle burn."

THE FIRST TIME Pickle and I traveled off-island so she could participate in a gymnastics meet was a special day: a journey of father and daughter into the maw of competition, driving to a faraway town where other little girls in pigtails and glitter would stand in the way of our quest for blue ribbons, little trophies, and complete gymnastics domination. Pickle was seven years old.

"Daddy, it's not like that," she said, as I attempted to explain the finer points of the hard-stare and tough-guy swagger. "Remember," she advised me, "people we don't know are just friends we haven't met yet." She was dressed in a purple leotard.

"Oh yeah," I said. "I keep forgetting that part. Could you at least growl for me? Just once?"

Pickle growled . . . and then blew me a kiss. I shrugged and we walked to the car. I brought a bag of stuffed animals, which I spread out across the backseat to "chase away the butterflies" in Pickle's stomach. I also brought three Taylor Swift CDs and a bag of snacks. We picked up Pickle's friend Maeve and mom Caitlin and the four of us drove to the ferry blasting T. Swift, singing out loud and pumping the air with our fists: *Losing him was blue, like I'd never known, / missing him was dark grey, all alone . . . but loving him was red, burning red.*

Taylor Swift is a *long* way from AC/DC—*She was a fast machine, she kept her motor clean / She was the best damn woman that I ever seen*—but being in the car with the music blasting, driving to my daughter's first big athletic competition, sent me back in time: Suddenly, I was in the passenger seat and my father was driving, the two of us on the road together almost every Saturday and Sunday as he took me to off-season wrestling matches up and down the state of New Jersey. We rolled a bit differently then. Our trips were intense affairs; I didn't even let my dad stop for coffee because I would be cutting weight, seated next to him encased in sweats and a plastic suit, maybe even spitting into a cup trying to squeeze out the last quarter pound before weigh-ins. There was no stuffed animals or coloring books, and I certainly wasn't thinking about making friends. Instead, I sat silently for most of the ride, cursing some kid I'd never met for making me lose weight, and planning my quick and decisive revenge on the mat.

My dad didn't know much about wrestling and I liked that because he was unable to give me too much advice. He was mostly my chauffeur, as all parents become at some stage of parenting. But once one of my matches started, my father became my self-appointed corner man shouting encouragement. During the regular season, my actual coach would be in the corner, but there were no coaches allowed in the off-season. I can still see my father standing on the edge of the thick foam mat, the normally quiet guy around the house suddenly transformed and yelling as loud as he could: "Attaboy, Billy! Attaboy!" Between periods he would towel me off, wiping the sweat from my forehead and shoulders, our bodies closer and more intimate than at any other time

I can recall. And at the end of each match, after the referee had raised my hand into the air, I would walk slowly toward my father so I could enjoy his wide smile and hear him say, "Good job, son. *Good job.*"

No such luck at a gymnastics meet.

At Pickle's gymnastics meet, the parents were sent to a small room off to the side of the competition area while the kids went through a door reserved for participants and coaches. I imagined that in the private room, the little girls braided their hair, took sips from their water bottles, and received last-minute advice from their coaches. Perhaps some even made friends as Pickle hoped. But I had no idea really, because I had my face pressed against a large window looking out into an empty gym waiting to see my girl emerge. The window was crowded with the eager faces of other parents, mostly moms but a few dads, too. The dad beside me sounded like he was whimpering, and I thought about offering him a hug.

Eventually, the parents were herded from the small room and out into the gym. We jockeyed for prime seats in the bleachers. It was a holiday meet and John Lennon's "Happy Xmas (War Is Over)" played as the girls entered the gym. There were perhaps one hundred kids scurrying about, testing the springy floor, the balance beam, bars, the pommel horse. Older kids waded into the stands and hawked Gym-o-Grams, where you wished your child good luck on a note-card and it was read over the loudspeaker. I bought five—a few under assumed names such as "Mr. Pushups says 'Stay tough, Pickle!'"—hoping she'd hear them and look over at me in the stands. But it was a one-way street, just me looking out at her, and an odd feeling overtook me as I watched her every move. I realized that I was *always* watching her, that in some ways that felt like my primary role as her father: looking at her and making sure she was okay. But now I was stranded in an anonymous sea of parents. It was a distant feeling, one that crept up my spine and landed with a lump in my throat the size of the ferryboat.

I stood and began waving frantically and calling out "Pickle! Pickle!" Each time I said her name I felt on the verge of tears. Finally, she looked over at me and gave me a small, quick wave as if to say, "Please calm down, you old fool."

And with that I did sit back down, comfortable in the knowledge that she knew where I was and also that I knew nothing about gymnastics and could only yell with wild encouragement: "Attagirl, Pickle! Attagirl!" But oh how I wished I could leave the bleachers to be her corner man.

AFTER THE MEET, driving toward home, we were both quiet in the car and it occurred to me that I had no recollection of the rides home after my wrestling meets. Maybe my father and I were mostly silent, too, tired and reflecting on the day's events. It was a good feeling, the contented silence, and I glanced at Pickle in the rear-view mirror, her awards ribbons in one hand and her security blanket in the other—she was at once a very little girl and growing older with each mile we traveled.

"Hey, Pickle," I said.

"Yes, Dad?"

"How about we stop and visit your grandfather on the way home?"

"What for?"

"Oh, I don't know . . . I just want to say hi."

28.

For a time, Pickle had trouble going to sleep. "There are nightmares waiting out there," she told me. "Werewolves, wide-open spaces, and scary marionettes!"

One night, to soothe her, I lay down beside her, a night-light glowing from the corner of the room, and I told her about what I did as a boy to calm my nerves at night.

"I would imagine an enormous bug," I told her.

I'm not sure where the idea came from, but the bug was huge, the size of a few houses stacked together. And all the kids would run to the bug after school and climb a ladder that stretched from the ground to the bug's back, which was hidden from the world of adults and all things that were scary. It was a huge playground up there, with everything kids liked to do: play baseball and badminton, paint pictures, swing on swings, eat candy and cupcakes. It was a free-for-all, and everyone was happy up there on top of this giant but genial bug.

"It always worked," I said. "I conjured up this Shangri-La so I could drift off to sleep with a smile on my face."

The memory comforted me again and I turned to Pickle, pleased with myself for remembering to share this story with her.

But her eyes were open wide, her face contorted.

"A giant bug!?" she shrieked. "What is wrong with you? Can you please leave and tell Mom to come in."

29.

～～～

DAY WAS MY daughter's security blanket, a small square of blue felt with a satin border she liked to move her fingers along like a set of worry beads. We weren't positive about how the blanket got its name, but we thought it started when Pickle was a baby and Cathlin would come home from work, sit down to nurse, and ask her, "How was your day?"

Day had a boomerang life, periodically getting lost and then resurfacing sometimes as much as a year later. Once, Day lay undisturbed beneath a bed at Grandma's house for about five months before a late-summer cleaning spree unearthed it. During preschool, Day disappeared for more than a year, lost somewhere in Aquinnah on the far western end of Martha's Vineyard. I thought I knew where we'd lost Day, while hiking, and retraced our steps many times before I stopped, stood at the top of the cliffs looking out to sea, and accepted my failure as a father as I imagined the impending doom of many sleepless nights.

During Day's long absence, we developed a new bedtime ritual, a version of counting sheep but with a lot more variety, to take the place of snuggling with Day. While I scratched Pickle's back, I had to come up with a new animal for her to count each night. Repeats were allowed but only under a conditional basis, one that Pickle ruled over with an arbitrary hand. At some point in this process, Pickle rolled over on her back and lifted her arm over her head. Without hesitation, I put my forehead in her armpit. She counted out loud to five and then said, "Okay, I'm ready for sleep." It was the sort of thing you never read about in a parenting book or magazine, but it worked. For many years, I put my forehead in Pickle's armpit for five seconds every night.

A year after losing Day, I was back by the Aquinnah Cliffs grabbing a fish taco at Faith's Fish Shack when I spotted the familiar blue blanket on the counter, hanging out as if part of the food crew. I whooped and clapped and cried I was so happy to see it. The owner's daughter had gone to preschool with Pickle and evidently recognized the blanket when she found it lying on the ground but I guess didn't tell anyone who it belonged to and so Day just hung around at the café, perhaps used occasionally as a dishrag but otherwise not too much worse for wear. When I presented the blanket to Pickle that afternoon, I expected a hero's welcome for finally finding her beloved security blanket. Instead, Pickle just shrugged as though the absence had been merely a matter of hours. She was, I realized, changing every day in ways I couldn't even see.

EVENTUALLY, PICKLE FOUND a substitute set of talismans: a wooden stake whittled to a point by Hardy, a bottle of holy water, and a cross. We had started watching *Buffy the Vampire Slayer* together and she fancied herself a slayer, too.

One day, she suggested we take a walk down Snake Hollow Road, across from the Tashmoo Overlook.

"I don't *trust* that road," she told me.

We went at dusk, parking at the overlook and then walking hand in hand down the dark wooded road. Pickle carried a green purse, which held her stake, cross, and holy water. The walk was uneventful, no vampires or even snakes, but we planned to go back soon.

Hardy had no interest in watching *Buffy*, so the two of us watched a much different 1990s television icon: *Twin Peaks*. The last time I'd watched that surreal show had been almost thirty years earlier, when I was in my twenties and living on the corner of 35th Street and 9th Avenue in a New York City neighborhood so abandoned it didn't even have a scary name like its neighbor to the north, Hell's Kitchen. A mysterious blow-dart attacker roamed the neighborhood, and most nights I drank too much as I hid from the person I wanted to be. While we watched *Twin Peaks*, I stole glances at Hardy and marveled that the teenager next to me was the same person I once rocked to sleep in the delivery room on the day he was born.

AT SOME POINT, I realized Pickle had become my security blanket. Walking hand in hand with her, as I had with Hardy when he was younger, I felt like her protector and that I was protected, too. Pickle's small hand in mine was all I needed to feel whole. But handholding, especially entering a new school year, becomes an uncertain thing. Hardy had begun denying me handholding at the start of second grade and I wasn't sure what to expect from Pickle on her first day of third grade.

I was happy as we entered the classroom hand in hand that day. We checked in with her new teacher, and after putting Pickle's things in her cubby, the teacher showed us a jar with a chrysalis hanging from the top. "It will be a monarch butterfly in a few days," she said. The next day there was another jar with three caterpillars crawling around on twigs and munching leaves. A few days later, they too morphed into chrysalises.

I became obsessed with these small green orbs, hanging from the tops of their jars. They seemed so fragile, holding on by just a wisp, but quietly powerful, doing nothing to the naked eye but behind the scenes changing completely. Each morning at dropoff, I stared at them while Pickle and her friends milled about the classroom.

It took about a week for the butterflies to emerge. I wasn't there when it happened, but Pickle told me about it in great detail, how the butterflies appeared seemingly out of nowhere, fully grown and with beautiful wings, and how the entire class went outside to set them free. As Pickle described the moment, I imagined the butterflies soaring above the playground, neither lingering nor looking back. Instead, they just lifted into the air, proud of their new wings and bodies as they disappeared forever into the trees. I wished them safe travels, clear of predators, be it birds, vampires, or the passage of time. I also recalled something I said to Pickle in second grade: I told her she was the perfect age and that I would prefer it if she stopped getting older. It was an offhand dad joke, but wrapped up with the real feelings of a dad who deep down didn't want his daughter to grow up.

Later that same day, I heard Pickle talking to Cathlin and crying. "Dad doesn't want me to get older," she sobbed, "but I can't help it."

I never again said out loud that I wanted Pickle to stop growing up, though I thought about it almost every day—especially when halfway through third grade, Pickle told me I could no longer hold her hand when we walked into school.

30.

~~~~~~~

ONE MORNING AT the breakfast table, Pickle told me about a young girl in her class who had the best late-for-school excuse.

"My friend and her father stopped to watch a group of ring-necked pheasants," Pickle said. "They actually wrote that down on the tardy slip: *Stopped to watch a group of ring-necked pheasants.*"

I smiled and imagined a lovely father–daughter scene at the edge of the woods before school. For a moment I thought about going in search of pheasants or other woodland creatures with Pickle, about how we could pile up a stack of wildlife-watching late-for-school slips throughout the year. Then I looked at the clock.

"Oh no, we're running late," I said.

And just like that the calm was broken and the morning turned into a chaos of arguments over tooth-brushing mishaps, misplaced homework, sneakers-versus-shoes and other wardrobe malfunctions. The argument reached such a pitch that by the time we got to the car, neither of us was speaking to the other and all thoughts about the magical properties of nature had been abandoned. We drove to school in silence, something that rarely happened.

At her drop-off spot, I turned to Pickle and attempted a last-minute reconciliation joke.

"Hey, how about I write you a note saying you're late because you had a fight with your father?"

Pickle didn't crack a smile. She just shook her head as she slid out of the car and closed the door.

As I drove on alone toward work, I passed a cluster of rabbits, some lovely birds, and two deer. I gave them all the finger.

31.

~~~~~

HARDY AND PICKLE have all but grown up in the *Vineyard Gazette* newsroom. Many days, I'd push back from my desk in the early afternoon, walk the three blocks to the Whaling Church, and wait for their school bus while I sat beside the wide white pillars of the church.

The kids and I would walk hand in hand from the bus stop to the *Gazette*, their backpacks thumping, their feet seeking puddles to splash in.

After I made them a snack, Hardy would settle into a chair in the corner of the newsroom to bury his nose in a book. Pickle would claim an empty desk, one usually reserved for a summer intern but vacant in the off-season. She would then reach into the desk drawer where she kept a pad and pencil and call downstairs to Jared or Jane in the graphics department to interview them about their day.

When the police scanner crackled, everyone stopped writing and talking to listen. Often it was a benign call about a stray dog or cat, although once a naked bicyclist was causing a scene downtown. Other times it could be a much more serious story. During the busy summer months, when the narrow roads became crowded with all manner of drivers, car accidents were more common. In the off-season there were even darker stories, such as domestic disputes and overdoses—the real muck of life. And occasionally there were bodies uncovered, such as one discovered in the state forest.

Pickle was there in the *Gazette* newsroom the day the dispatcher's voice on the scanner reported the dead body in the woods. She began to cry. I took her by the hand and walked her downstairs and out the door to find an open café to get her a cup of hot cocoa. As we walked, I wondered, as I often did, about exposing her to cruel facts of life, just as I wondered about the stories Cathlin and I shared at the dinner table. Sometimes the result of a scanner announcement became a memorial service for Cathlin to perform. But this was our lives. Cathlin and I were uniquely stationed as witnesses to real life in our respective jobs, so we chose not to censor but instead to talk about these moments with Hardy and Pickle, whether at the dinner table or over hot cocoa with marshmallows while sitting on a bench beside the harbor as the gulls circled overhead and the work back in the newsroom just had to wait.

We also looked for ways for the children to directly interact with the complexities of real life, such as the time Pickle and I took a road trip when she was eight years old to attend the 2017 Women's March in Washington, D.C.

Pickle's real name, Eirene, means *peace* in biblical Greek, a language Cathlin studied at seminary. The name Eirene and its meaning have always loomed large for me, and in a way I was happy not to use it when Pickle was young. But while driving down to the Women's March, she asked me if we could use her given name for the weekend.

"Of course," I said. "It feels right to me, too."

It's a twelve-hour drive from Martha's Vineyard to Washington, D.C. We stopped many times, including at the Clara Barton Service Area, the last rest stop in New Jersey before crossing over to Delaware. While picking out snacks, we bumped into Rose Styron, Jenny Allen, and Brooke and Lynne Adams, from the Vineyard. They were also on their way to the march, but bumping into them at a random rest stop was a bizarre coincidence and we marveled at it. Rose was fired up—an experienced activist in her eighties, it never occurred to her to sit this one out.

On Saturday morning, the line to get into the subway station was so long it took an hour just to get to the turnstiles; that was my first realization of just how large the march would be. Eirene quickly made friends with a couple from upstate New York. The man wore a tie with lots of tiny panda bears on it, and Eirene smiled and told him how much she liked it.

"I bought it in China," he told her.

Then the man turned to me and said that many years ago they had adopted two young girls from China. The girls were in high school, and after Trump's election some kids at school began telling them to go back to China, where they belonged.

"That's not the country I thought I was living in," the man said. "That's why we're here today."

Eirene stood by my side, listening but not responding.

Coming up out of the subway we saw a policeman. He smiled at everyone, waved, and said, "Happy protesting!"

Cathlin's one bit of advice before we left home was to stay away from people with masks. "They may do things you don't want to be a part of," she explained to Eirene.

We didn't see any marchers with masks, but Eirene asked me if she should avoid people with "naughty words" on their signs.

"I don't think that's possible," I said, as the signs were everywhere and ranged from the political to the humorous to a wide range of references about the female anatomy. I deferred all questions about this new vocabulary to when we returned home to Mom.

I didn't grow up a marcher and had remained on the sidelines until I met Cathlin, who attended her first march as an eight-year-old standing side by side with her mother at a No Nukes rally in Battery Park. My first march was in Philadelphia with Cathlin, for a cause I can't remember. The only thing I remember is that Jackson Browne walked with our very small group, and we were told we couldn't touch his hair. Before hearing this I had never considered touching Jackson Browne's hair, but after being told not to, it was all I could think about.

We couldn't see or hear the speeches at the march. There were too many people. But it didn't matter. Walking among the crowds was enough—or rather it was more than enough. I watched Pickle watch all of the women around us. They had gray hair, they pushed strollers, they wore braces on their teeth and streaks of color in their hair. They did gymnastics and handstands, they hobbled on canes. Some were topless and a few were naked. There were men, too, but women were the clear majority by hundreds of thousands. Smiling and kindness ruled the day and it was a glimpse, I felt, of what the world might be if women had all the power and men simply stood on the sidelines cheering and chanting "Her Body, Her Choice."

We stayed at the march for eight hours, taking a short break in the National Gallery, which flanks the National Mall. A few days before we set out on our road trip, Eirene told me Monet was her favorite artist. This was news to me. But soon after entering the gallery, she yelled "Monet!" and ran to look at some of the artist's paintings. I felt unmoored for a moment as I watched my daughter stand with a group of marchers taking a time out for art. It was as though I could see her for the first time as a woman and as an individual.

THE DAY AFTER the march, on the drive home, the traffic was unbearable as so many people tried to leave the city at once. It took us seven hours to go a hundred miles. At one rest stop, while Eirene and I stood by the car stretching, a group of young women were doing a dance routine to get their own blood flowing. One of them waved, then walked over to us. She pointed to our Massachusetts license plate and said she was from Stockbridge.

Soon a crowd formed as other cars filled with marchers driving home stopped to take a break. We all stood together, stretching and talking and marveling not just at the number of people who attended the rally but also about the spirit of goodwill and kindness that overflowed from everyone.

Later, when friends back home asked Eirene what her favorite part of the march was, she always gave a different answer: meeting so many people, the friendly policeman, the dogs wearing pink hats with cat ears, standing on the steps of the National Gallery and looking out at the crowds, seeing a Monet painting, reading so many naughty words.

I, too, had many favorite moments from the weekend. And yet it was that Sunday at the rest stop, trying to escape bumper-to-bumper traffic, I think of most when I think of the march.

It never seemed odd that a large group of strangers had gathered to talk at a roadside rest stop, because after the march we'd all just experienced together, in many ways we weren't strangers. I introduced my daughter to everyone as Eirene and explained what her name meant. And when I close my eyes, I can still see our new friends cheering for her against the backdrop of gas pumps, parked cars, and a Wendy's sign—especially me, who had taken a step back to watch my daughter shine.

32.

~~~~~

PREDAWN BREAKFASTS ON Sundays might not be the
norm for most households, but for ministers they're stan-
dard operating procedure. On a Sunday morning in Georgia
in 2015, I sat with Cathlin at 5:30 drinking a cup of coffee
while she sipped at her half a cup of tea. Adrenaline had her
mostly wide awake. Our host, Reverend Raphael Warnock,
stood by the kitchen sink, also drinking tea.

Cathlin and Reverend Warnock met at Union Seminary
in New York City when they were both in their twenties
and formed a deep friendship. When we moved to Martha's
Vineyard, Cathlin convinced Raphael to visit and to preach
at her church. He soon began to come every summer, and his
sermons continue to be an annual highlight at the First Congregational Church of West Tisbury. He became something
of a second minister there. Eventually, he invited Cathlin to
preach to his congregation, the Ebenezer Baptist Church in
Atlanta, the spiritual home of Dr. Martin Luther King Jr.

This was years before Reverend Warnock decided to run
for U.S. Senate, when we would return to Atlanta to walk
side by side with him during the 2020 runoff election. When
we would share takeout dinners with an exhausted and en-

ergized candidate after a day of knocking on doors to get out the vote.

That future was not on our minds in 2015. But Cathlin preaching to more than two thousand people in such a historic church certainly was, along with the honor and nerves of the occasion.

"You know what one of my congregants does every week to tell me she loves me?" Raphael asked, as we finished our coffee and tea and prepared to leave for the church. "She's an elderly woman, and each week after I preach she gives me a big chocolate bar. You know, like, 'Good job, Raphael, here's your candy bar!'"

"She's Mom-ing you," Cathlin said with a smile.

"Amen to that," Raphael said.

Cathlin and I had been in Atlanta for three days, staying with Raphael and taking in the city. When we drove around, I sat in the backseat of his car so the ministers could talk up front. Cathlin repeatedly offered me the front seat, but I declined. They're old friends and I loved seeing them together, reminiscing and laughing and lowering their voices to discuss the difficulties of being a minister: talking people through addiction, sadness, loneliness, injustice, divorce, the death of a loved one, and, of course, the burying of that loved one.

"We hold people's pain," Raphael said, summing up one of their conversations.

"Amen to that," Cathlin said.

"You got your manuscript?" Raphael asked Cathlin as we walked out the door of his home. "You ready to preach the gospel?"

It was a fifteen-minute drive to Ebenezer. Along the way we passed by Dr. King's birth home. In fact, the whole area around the church is a historic landmark, and tourists come daily to walk this trail through history.

One of Raphael's deacons greeted us in the parking lot, led us into the church, up the elevator, and into Raphael's office. While I looked at pictures on the wall of Raphael and various local and national dignitaries, including President Obama, his secretary knocked on the door. "The senator is here," she said.

"The senator" was Leroy Johnson, once one of the most powerful men in the South. Senator Johnson was the first Black man elected to the Georgia Senate after Reconstruction. When Muhammad Ali had his boxing license revoked because of his stance against the war in Vietnam, it was Senator Johnson who arranged his return to the ring with a fight in Georgia.

The senator greeted us and spent a few moments with Cathlin, thanking her for coming. He told her, "I know you'll be wonderful," and something about the way he said it was empowering, as though with a wave of his hand he could make it so.

After the senator left, Cathlin and I formed a circle with Raphael and he said a prayer. I looked over at Cathlin with her head bowed, and it was her white skin, something I usually take for granted, just like my own, that caught my eye. There was no getting around the issue of race in that moment. For Cathlin and Raphael, friendship and a shared vision of how to help the most needy among us were the defining characteristics of their relationship. But from the outside, the image of a Black Baptist preacher and a white

Congregationalist minister standing together at the pulpit meant something more, the significance of which they were just beginning to understand, Cathlin often told me.

Cathlin had prepared a sermon about friendship, told through the lens of her long history with Raphael and the role of prophetic friendships throughout time. Her story would include how in seminary she and Raphael had led a protest by ministers in 1999, wearing their robes down at city hall in New York after the killing of Amadou Diallo, an unarmed immigrant from Guinea who was shot forty-one times by the police. Some things have changed, Cathlin would say in her sermon, while others have not: *We are a people too quick to pull the trigger, to exert power over another.*

Just before the service, we were escorted to the sanctuary, where the energy was already electric, the choir was rocking, and a young minister warmed up the crowd. Cathlin and Raphael headed to the pulpit and a deacon led me to a seat. He suggested the first row, but I motioned toward the second. The deacon paused for a moment as if not sure how to handle the situation. I was confused, too: What was one row or another? Then the deacon told me quietly that I could have the second row, but I couldn't sit on the aisle as that spot was reserved. Later, an elderly Black woman, escorted by two other women, sat in that spot. It was Martin Luther King Jr.'s sister, Christine King Farris, whom everyone calls Miss Sissy. During the service, another one of Dr. King's relatives, his sister-in-law, gave me a big hug and kissed both of my cheeks. A welcoming warmth radiated from everyone around me.

When it was time for the sermon, Raphael introduced Cathlin by talking about their long history together. He called her "a dear friend with a righteous rap sheet," a reference to the many times she has been arrested for standing up to injustice. At home, we have a picture of Cathlin wearing a beret and seated in the back of a paddy wagon with other protesters. We once showed the photo to the children as an example of their mother's life before them, but it frightened Pickle so much, this glimpse of her mother going to jail for what she believed in, that we had to put it away.

Since it was Earth Day Sunday at Ebenezer, Cathlin had been asked to weave the environment into her sermon. She quoted from Dr. King's sermon about the levels of love that humans experience, from friendship to humanitarian to agape love, the highest form because, he had preached, "it is the love of God operating in the human heart. And it comes to the point that you even love the enemy." She took the congregation through the levels of love to look at how humans should strive to treat one another, and then through this same lens she painted a picture of her relationship to the earth: *"For forty-six years, I have crawled, toddled and walked on this planet. Driven, biked, hiked and run upon this planet. But how well do I really know it? We love a sunset on the beach or a rainbow after a storm. We love the earth for the aesthetic gifts it offers. We may notice the earth, but do we invest any real time in getting to know her. Does this even merit a level of love? Dr. King might call this the utilitarian level. I love the earth for what it gives to me. Is this a classic case of the oppressor ignoring the demands of the oppressed?"*

A few of Cathlin's congregants once told her they sometimes have a tough time going to church because they often end up crying and would rather not do that in public. Cathlin seemed confused by this, but I understood: she holds people's pain, even in her sermons. She allows people to sit, for at least a moment, with their lives and their struggles—but perhaps even more important, her own vulnerability and hopefulness are always on display, allowing others to feel more deeply too: *"It is true of friends that they call forth more from us. They believe in us when we are full of doubt. They introduce us to new possibilities for growth and learning. They show us new people and experiences. Just look at this opportunity to preach before you this morning. Reverend Warnock has stretched what is possible for me."*

Cathlin has no ego, at least not one that I have been able to discern in all the decades I've known her. I think this more than anything else is what makes her an exceptional minister and preacher. She doesn't seek center stage, yet each week that's exactly where she stands. And in Atlanta, that stage was very large.

AFTER PREACHING TWO services at Ebenezer Baptist Church, one at eight in the morning and another at eleven, Cathlin stood in a receiving line with Raphael, greeting the congregation. Many stopped to speak with her and thank her, and a few said they were headed to the Vineyard over the summer and would see her there. The candy bar woman had two pieces of chocolate: one for Raphael and one for Cathlin.

Once the church emptied, Raphael, Cathlin, and I prepared to head back to his house for a quick rest before he had to return to the church to lead a memorial service for a much-loved congregant who had died in a car accident. The sermon and Sunday service were over, but now, as Cathlin and Raphael often said, the real work of the week would begin.

33.

O N THE ISLAND, the grammar schools feed into a large regional high school and a small public charter school. Whenever I tell people the annual graduating class at the regional high school is around 160 students, they look at me with surprise. Some are shocked to learn there's a high school at all, while others had imagined something tiny, perhaps tucked away in the woods or near a beach.

Before Hardy's freshman year, Cathlin and I drove to the high school for an orientation, along with the parents of all the other kids. Entering the school, we encountered a banner that read WELCOME TO THE CLASS OF 2022.

We shuffled into the auditorium, having been there for events during the years—dance recitals, plays, concerts during the summer. But this was different; this was a whole new stage of life for our kids. I tried to listen to the principal talk about what high school meant for our children, and the academics and extracurricular activities that awaited them. But my mind kept wandering to the hallways of my New Jersey high school, to scurrying from class to class as a freshman. Hardy was leaving the womb of elementary school, and so were we. No longer would we be able to chart the entire course of his life. His independence was about to grow, along with the influence of others.

And so while I sat shoulder to shoulder with my fellow parents, I was also standing on the side of a wrestling mat, staring at my high school hero who'd recently had his ear chewed off in a fight in the parking lot of the Four Roses Bar.

THE FOUR ROSES was a last-stop type of bar on the side of Route 22, a crowded, cranky highway that stretches from Newark, New Jersey, to somewhere deep in Pennsylvania. It had a blinking neon sign with the outline of a red rose, and a parking lot big enough for short-haul trucks and lots of motorcycles.

I wasn't there the night of the fight between Jeff Hoffman, the captain of my wrestling team, and some nameless and faceless truckers. Even a place like the Four Roses wouldn't let a skinny fourteen-year-old kid in the door. But I like to think that if I had been there, I somehow could've stopped it.

When Jeff was our captain, he was a senior stud with arms as big as seaplane pontoons. I was at the other end of the spectrum, an eighty-three-pounder with puberty still mocking me from a far horizon. I had been considered tough in middle school, but high school was another world, where men like Jeff ruled. For a time, he was everything I wanted to be.

Our first match that year was against Middlesex, a town a few miles down Route 22. I stood at the edge of the mat quaking as I stared at my opponent, a hairy-chested dude with a shaved head and a chipped front tooth. He looked meaner and tougher than any opponent I'd ever faced, and in no time he proved it. When the whistle blew, he grabbed my head and stuck it in his armpit just because he could. He smelled like stick-shift muscle cars, school suspensions, and a broken home.

He pinned me in less than a minute.

I came off the mat with my head hung low to hide my tears and slumped down on the bench. Jeff kneeled in front of me so he could look at me eye to eye.

"Hey," he said. "Don't sweat it. Let me show you how it's done."

Then he stood and walked toward the mat as if savoring every step.

Jeff played to the crowd, not crushing his opponents quickly but toying with them, lifting them high in the air and locking them into painful positions. His matches usually ended with a pin or lopsided score and only rarely was it close. Once in a great while, Jeff lost. On those occasions, I didn't know what to do and just stared at my hero, bathed in sweat, his muscles inflated from exertion, his face buried in his hands while he sat silently at the end of the bench. I imagine it was after one of those losses that Jeff visited the Four Roses Bar and said the wrong words to the wrong group of men.

I watched Jeff obsessively when I was a freshman. I learned his path through the hallways and sometimes followed at a distance, studying the group of girls who always trailed him, the heavy scent of lip gloss surrounding them like a moat too wide to cross. I found out where he lived and on nightly jogs through town I'd pass his house, along with other homes of people I was interested in—a girl I had a crush on, a teacher, my friends and my rivals. Our town was neither rich nor poor, so the shapes and sizes of the homes didn't differ much. But for me, pausing at night to watch how the light shined from the windows, how a door stood solid or fragile, the lawns lush or left to fend for themselves, I felt I better understood these people who for a time meant everything to me.

A few weeks into the wrestling season, I won my first varsity match. Jeff greeted me when I walked off the mat by grabbing me and lifting me into the air, turning me slowly a full 360 degrees so that everyone in the gym could see me and I could see them, standing and cheering and stomping the bleachers.

I can't remember how long Jeff was absent from school after the fight or how many times that week I reached up to feel my own two ears, trying to imagine what took place that night. When Jeff eventually returned, I didn't ask him any details about the Four Roses. Instead, I joined the rest of team in asking to see the result of the fight. Jeff shrugged and pulled back his hair, revealing a small mound where an ear should have been. We all groaned. I stepped back, whereas others lingered and leaned forward inspecting, and perhaps reveling in, every detail. Not everyone revered Jeff as I did. This was high school, after all, and he had enemies, even on the team, other upperclassmen who resented him, perhaps because he was cocky, or for other more complicated reasons I had no clue about. I was just a freshman, still wide-eyed to the nuances of high school dynamics. But I was about to learn how cruel we could all be.

Later that week, as we rolled out the mats in the gym, getting ready for our next match, I looked to the wall where the roster of wrestlers hung. But instead of a list of our names, someone had moved the letters around to read: "Hoffman Has No Ear, Ha, Ha."

I wish I had said or done something then to come to Jeff's defense as he walked into the gym and saw what a teammate had done. Instead, I just watched as Jeff shrugged again like he had when he first revealed his ear. He didn't get mad or yell or ask who was responsible. And when my other team-mates laughed, I laughed. too.

It's always perplexing to me which memories attach themselves. That moment laughing awkwardly in the gym-nasium when I was a freshman in high school doesn't rank anywhere near the worst things I did as a young boy. And yet it stays with me as a moment in time when I was trying so hard to figure out what sort of man I wanted to be, and often fell far short.

A WEEK OR so after Hardy's freshman orientation, I taught him how to shave. It wasn't a long lesson, just a bit of shav-ing cream on his upper lip and a few swipes of the razor to clear away the small line of dark hairs that had recently appeared.

As I stood in the bathroom with Hardy, watching him hold the razor with confidence, staring at his reflection, I saw myself in a similar bathroom with my father standing behind me. And then the image widened to include Jeff Hoffman lifting me in the air after my first victory. That image gave way to a long line of memories of father figures who had traveled in and out of my life. I wanted so badly to tell Hardy about what I was seeing, about the boy I was and the man I had become, and my hope that this combination would be enough to help the two us during his high school years, when joy and cruelty so often walk hand in hand, along with confusion and wonder. But in the moment, I had no idea how to put words to these feelings. As in high school, words failed me.

Instead, I pointed to his lip and said, "You missed a spot."

34.

WHEN YOU'RE ALONE in your house—your family gone for almost two months—the stuffed animals really begin to stand out. The silence is there, too, awkward and endless, but you expect that. It's the steady stares of the pink elephant and the snuggly rabbit that sneak up on you—stuffed animals are cute when accompanied by small children, but otherwise downright disturbing.

In the fall of 2015, when Pickle was eight and Hardy was eleven, Cathlin took a four-month sabbatical from her church and received a grant from the Louisville Institute to spend it in Scotland. She went alone for the month of September and then I visited with the kids for two weeks in October. When I returned to the Vineyard for work, the kids stayed in Scotland with Cathlin.

While waiting for my flight home in the Glasgow airport, I passed a toy store with a man out front dressed up as a giant green dog. He was goofing around with some kids, enticing them with bubble machines and other knickknacks sold in the store. By reflex I began walking toward him, this six-foot talking dog wearing white gloves and doing magic tricks—it's what you do when you have small children. But then I remembered that I was alone, not a father being tugged forward by his kids. I quickly turned around and walked away before any of the parents noticed me; there are probably laws, I thought, against single men cheering on giant dog magicians surrounded by small kids.

BACK HOME ON the island, I soon realized that not only were my children missing, but also the whole routine of my life felt as though it had been erased. I didn't need to go to school dropoffs, so I didn't see my circle of parent friends or my children's friends. I didn't go to story hours at the library, ballet classes, or tennis lessons. I enjoyed not spending hours each day organizing playdates or surviving harried mornings making school lunches. But I began to grow uneasy when I noticed by the second or third day alone that I was no longer experiencing my full range of emotions either. Although I had never realized it, before children I lived life in the middle ground of emotions, never fully venturing out to the extremes. I never felt I'd lost my temper until I encountered my son having a full-blown tantrum about which socks to wear. I never felt true contentment until I sat between my son and daughter reading them books I loved as a child. I never experienced how deep love—or exhaustion—could be.

While alone, I felt myself returning to a smaller playing field of emotions. Yet without the moment-to-moment scrum of parental survival, I could somehow see and love my children more clearly. The feeling was disconcerting: *Could I really be a better father in absentia?*

At the end of the first week, to combat the loneliness, in the evening I went for a drive. A few miles down the road I passed

Cathlin's church and saw people headed inside for the weekly community supper. Food insecurity is a big issue on the island and so is loneliness in the off-season. Therefore, the churches around the island got together and split up the week to ensure that anyone could find a free meal and some company every night of the week. Cathlin's community suppers were on Wednesday evenings, and I often drove over after work.

Although the meal was free, it wasn't simply a soup kitchen. It was a gathering, a breaking of bread together. Seniors looking to get out of the house attended, as did parents happy not to cook for the evening. Everyone sat at long tables arranged around the parish hall. One night, I looked around the room and saw a landscaper who used to watch over my grandmother many years ago. I waved to him and remembered that he used to salute my grandmother whenever he left for the day. At the door he would turn, raise his fist in the air, and say to her: "Courage! Life takes courage."

Edward Hoagland often went to the community suppers, too, until he moved off-island a few years ago due to declining health. Hoagland is an incredible writer and someone I'd admired from afar for many years. When I learned he lived a just few blocks from the *Gazette*, staying the off-season in a house his father bought long ago and moving to Vermont in the summer, I immediately called him for an interview. As often happens on a small island, we went on to become friends. Eventually, I convinced him to write essays for the *Gazette*. He'd type them out, walk to the office, and put them in my mailbox. And if I didn't publish one right away, he'd pass a cryptic note to Pickle to give to me during the community supper: "When" it would say, or even more enigmatic "???"

Hoagland was almost blind, so every time I edited a piece I'd walk to his house and read it to him. This was a nerve-racking experience, reading my edits to a writer I admired so much and many years my senior as he sat a few feet from me, leaning forward in his chair to listen closely.

Once, after I had visited his house and gone over the edits, I made a few more edits back in the office. I thought they were small changes, nibbling away at some long sentences to make them more direct for the reader. When Hoagland read the final version in the newspaper, he left an angry note at the office, telling me that what I'd done was unprofessional and that he would never work with me again.

Hoagland was right, of course, I never should have published the piece without his final approval.

I walked to his house to apologize and try to make things right. I knocked on the door and he greeted me cordially, inviting me in for tea. I said I was sorry and explained that I had made the final small edits to help the readers find their way.

Hoagland shook his head. "I want my sentences to twist and turn so the reader has to work at them," he said. "It means they have to pay attention."

ANOTHER DAY, WHILE driving around, I noticed my daughter's Taylor Swift CD in the car, so I popped it in. Before long my mood shifted. I turned up the volume and sang along like Pickle: *I don't know about you / But I'm feelin' twenty-two / Everything will be alright if / You keep me next to you.*

For a moment it felt as if both my children were riding with me, Pickle adding harmony from the backseat and Hardy complaining about the choice of music. But as I belted out the chorus, I realized I had arrived at a stop sign . . . the car windows were down and my voice carried to a small crowd of tourists who looked at me and began to laugh. I tried to maintain my dignity by smiling and waving. It didn't work, so I raised the windows and drove off with a screech of tires.

On the way home, I switched to Bruce Springsteen's "You're Missing," another one of Pickle's favorites. The song is from *The Rising*, the album Bruce made in the aftermath of 9/11. It's a moving song, but a deeply sad one about a husband and father who won't be coming home ever again: *Everything is everything / Everything is everything / But you're missing.* The song was too much for me and I turned it off. As I drove in silence, I wondered why my eight-year-old daughter enjoyed that song so much.

I tried to shake the mood of the song, but it stayed with me. Back at home I thought again about the moment at the Glasgow airport when I said goodbye to my children. After boarding my flight, I settled into my seat and buckled up. Before children, I would have opened a book, looked to the movie listings, or settled in for a nap. Back then I wasn't afraid of flying. But having children changed this. Now when I buckled up, I thought of all I had to lose. During takeoffs I pay attention, sitting up straight, feeling the acceleration of the plane down the runway, absorbing every bump on the tarmac and nudge of the wind. If anything happens, I want to be present and thinking about my family. Once the plane is aloft, I can relax, order a drink, and turn on a trashy movie—I feel somehow safer high in the sky than at points of contact.

ONE NIGHT, NEAR the end of the sabbatical, I couldn't sleep and walked outside to look at the stars. When Pickle was very young, she decided I was the one who put the stars up in the sky each evening, climbing a very tall ladder and working deep into the night. When I put her to bed, she would quiz me about my task, asking *How did you get the job?* (A wood troll gave it to me as both a curse and a blessing.) *What's the hardest part?* (The top of the Big Dipper.) Pickle also decided that Calder, her friend Maeve's dad, took over the duties if I was sick.

When I said goodbye to Pickle in Scotland, she brought up my star-hanging, even though at age eight I was sure she didn't believe it anymore. While crying and hugging me, she reminded me of my job in the night sky. Then she suggested that I give Calder a call. "If you're lonely, you could put up the stars together," she offered, "and maybe add a few extra, since you'll have more time working as a team."

Pickle never told Calder that he was the relief star-dad, and I had never found the right moment to explain the situation to him either. But he was usually game for anything, so instead of returning to my quiet, empty house that evening, I drove over to his place.

And if you close your eyes, you can still see the two of us, along with so many other dads, standing tall on precarious ladders, trying so hard to be the guiding lights our children want us to be.

35.

～～

ONE WINTER PICKLE went on a sustained campaign to get a pet for Christmas. She wasn't fooling around; she talked of ponies and large dogs: malamutes, huskies, Great Danes.

Cathlin tried to bring her back to reality.

"How about a gerbil, dear?"

Pickle began to cry.

"A gerbil is a nice pet," Cathlin said.

Pickle cried harder and harder until she became inconsolable, walking around the house, her little shoulders heaving, head hung low, the sobs coming thick and loud. Usually, Pickle was such a mild-mannered sort. We tried to talk it through with her. She was so worked up that she could barely speak, but gradually her cries eased off, like a motor slowing down as it comes into the harbor.

"It's not nice . . ." she said between sniffles, ". . . for a Mommy to make up a fake animal when her daughter really wants a pet!"

My poor daughter, so deprived in her knowledge of the world of pets, didn't even know what a gerbil was. I felt like a bad father, because in truth, I knew it was me who was holding the parental line against bringing animals into the house. The irony is that I was the opposite of pet-deprived as a child. At various times, my brother and I owned dogs, cats, rabbits, gerbils, guinea pigs, boa constrictors, mice (to feed the snakes), a piranha, goldfish (to feed the piranha), turtles, chameleons, iguanas, and parakeets. When our parents said no to a monkey, my brother and I pouted for a week.

And the reason I kept saying no to Pickle's wish list of pets had almost nothing to do with the normal parental reservations, the added work and cost of another mouth to feed or fear of ticks. It had something to do with once being twenty-four years old and adrift in my own life. But how do you tell a little girl that her father was once not a pillar of strength—at least that's the impression I liked to think she had of me—but a mass of confusion? Much of my existence back then felt like walking in the pitch black, arms extended, searching but not knowing what I would bump into next and how much it would hurt. For a time, what I repeatedly bumped into was an animal.

I was living in New York City, the place so many of us swam to after college, hoping it would show us who we were supposed to be. I had majored in economics and begun working for a bank; I was following the path I thought I was supposed to. But I soon discovered I disliked working at a bank even more than I had disliked studying banking. After about a year, I quit and took the first job I could find, something I had heard about at a party: a nonprofit called New York Cares, which helped busy New Yorkers find volunteer opportunities such as tutoring, assisting at a soup kitchen, and cleaning a park. I loved that job, not so much for the work, which was mostly menial, but for how it began to transform my thinking. I finally gathered the courage to take my first writing class, something I had never done before, not in college or high school. But there was a downside, too. Although I was happy to give up my office cubicle and suit and tie, I also lost my half-decent paycheck and ability to pay the rent.

To survive, I began pet sitting in exchange for free places to stay. I lived this way for a year and a half, getting my fingers bitten by cranky birds and my bed visited by furry creatures of various sorts. These pets were not mine and there was never enough time to grow to love their idiosyncrasies. They were mere conduits to a lifestyle I didn't fully understand but which I took to with alarming gusto.

All my life I had played by the rules, acquired academic degrees and medals in ways my parents could brag about. While pet sitting, my parents didn't even know how to find me. Friends had a hard time, too, as these were the days when it was still possible to become lost or at least invisible, when there were no cell phones or Facebook to broadcast my trail. No one knew where I lived because I didn't either, not really. I changed apartments every few weeks. Keys were passed to me by doormen and secretaries, in lobbies, on street corners, and in subway stations. With each move I became a new me as I discovered my new neighborhood, new books, music, appliances, spices, plants, and, of course, pets.

Oh, Pickle, I wish you had known me back then, an explorer of sorts, who needed little more than a toothbrush and a subway token to survive.

For a few weeks I lived in the East Village on a listless street where each morning upon leaving the apartment I had to step over a man passed out on the sidewalk along with empty Chinese food containers and other garbage. The stench of urine was so strong that it felt like another tangible barrier on my way out the door. On the Upper West Side, I rejoiced among the brownstones and leafy avenues. I became one of the privileged while living in Gramercy Park and gaining access to its private garden. I explored Washington Heights, where, during a period in the 1980s, the neighborhood was ruled by a Dominican drug lord named El Feo—*The Ugly*. El Feo was gunned down in front of his bodega but rose to rule again from his wheelchair, only to be gunned down once again, this time for good. A neighbor told me the tale down in the laundry room. She had a bouffant hairdo on which a pet pigeon perched, bobbing its head in time to the rhythm of her voice.

Later, I moved to an apartment on 190th and Broadway, located directly above Ortiz's Funeral Home. It was summer, there was no air conditioning, and I was forced to keep the windows open even when blankets of embalming fluid floated through the window, covering everything in the business of death.

Pickle, can you keep a secret? I still think about that apartment above the funeral home with a fondness I can't explain.

I tried to resist being charmed by all the pets I met along the way, but I couldn't. Even the most frustrating animals I met are lodged in my memory, like Sophie, the country dog who, after moving to the city, refused to pee on asphalt and so I had to walk her deep into Riverside Park each night where frequently I would have to interrupt her business because I was about to get mugged. And Tom and Jerry, a pair of fiendish cats that woke me at all hours of the night as they rolled pencils across the hardwood floor, and no matter how much I searched, I could never find their stash.

It was a chaotic period but a time when I accepted that the only way to find out what came next was to begin taking random steps, even if on the surface they seemed to make no sense. If Pickle knew how fondly I looked back on those days, she would surely have been able to wrangle a pet out of me. She would only have needed to say: "Dad, tell me again about El Feo . . . and, by the way, can I keep this rabbit that followed me home?"

Pickle's pet crusade and my thinking about the past eventually took me further back, to when I was a young boy with a dog of my own. I was eleven years old, Jim and I sharing a small bedroom. We slept in bunk beds, he on the top and me on the bottom. Pushed against one wall were our two desks and on the opposite wall our two bureaus. We shared the poster space, too, my picture of Crazy Horse next to his poster of The Clash.

We also shared the family dog, a Labrador/spaniel mix named Triscuit—or so Jim and the rest of the family thought. In reality, my bond with Triscuit beat them all.

Every night at bedtime, Triscuit climbed onto my lower bunk bed. I would hold up the bedcovers and she would crawl in. She'd burrow deep down by my feet, curling up there and keeping my legs warm throughout the night. In the morning, I'd crawl down under the covers to lie next to her, the two of us transformed into a large lump at the end of the bed.

Triscuit was a spirited dog who cried inconsolably whenever we left her alone, then greeted us with a dance of joy when we returned. I knew that even the worst day in junior high would end with Triscuit's welcome home. After school, I often read while lying on the floor with my head resting on her stomach. She was only three years old but it was as if I couldn't remember life without her.

One morning I woke and heard Triscuit whimpering down by my feet. She thrashed for a moment and then went very still. The sheets down by my feet were soggy. I cursed her for wetting the bed and shoved her with my foot, but she didn't make a sound. I called her name but she didn't move. I peeled back the covers. Triscuit looked fine, still curled up in a ball, but she didn't respond. Then I noticed that her tongue was hanging loosely from her drooping mouth.

I began screaming. My father rushed into our room in his bathrobe. Moments later he ushered me silently out of the room.

I don't remember what happened to Triscuit's body; my father must have cleared it away without my seeing it. I don't remember going back to my room to change out of my pajamas for school, or standing in my room, looking at the bed, empty now and the wet sheets removed. I don't remember staring at the bed for a long time before my mother arrived to hug me and tell me she was very sorry, her eyes wet with tears. I don't remember my own tears, either. What I remember is never wanting another pet.

Oh, Pickle, I'm sorry. Perhaps you're right, and the time has come for your own furry friend to love.

Later, on Christmas morning, a Chinese dwarf hamster arrived in our home (best to start small). Seated by the fire, while Pickle played with her new pet, I told her a story about how her father was once a boy whose every bone ached with such sadness that he refused to take another chance, and how he eventually became a young man who found his sense of self while hopelessly lost among the beloved pets of strangers.

36.

A T THE EDGE of our yard, under the tree house, sits a chicken coop. For a long time, we had seven chickens. Every evening the chickens returned, hopped onto their roost, and huddled together. All that remained for me to do was to say "Goodnight, ladies," and shut the door.

One evening, when Pickle was ten years old, only five chickens returned at the end of the day. An hour after dusk a sixth returned, agitated and looking over her shoulder. I kept the coop door open for as long as I could while searching for the last chicken. Eventually, I gave up, knowing that even if the chicken was still alive, which seemed improbable, surviving the night would be impossible—raccoons lurked out there, ready to pounce.

I walked indoors with a heavy heart and told Pickle the news. She ran to the coop to see who was missing.

"It's Agnes," she said. "My *second favorite*!"

I was happy it wasn't Maybelle, the mellow chicken who would wander into the house and sit on our laps, or roost on the rocker on the front porch. I would have missed Maybelle, but far worse, Pickle would have been more devastated than she already was.

But Pickle started sobbing even harder, saying she felt guilty for being happy that a different chicken may have died. "I loved Agnes, *too*," she wailed, trying to navigate her conflicted feelings.

In the morning, I searched again through the underbrush surrounding the yard. After a few minutes, I found the body; Agnes had almost made it home.

I walked indoors and told Pickle the news.

"I *need* to see her," Pickle said.

"Are you sure?" I asked. "It's a hard thing to see."

"I'm sure," she said.

I stood back and watched Pickle pick her way into the underbrush. She looked so small among the trees and fallen leaves. The morning air was cold enough to sting my throat. I watched Pickle's back and narrow shoulders as she stopped, stood very still, and stared at the ground for a long time. She was getting older; I could feel it. She would be a teenager soon enough, I thought.

When Pickle came slowly out of the underbrush, I held out my hand to her. Then we walked together back to the house. I started to say something about how we had given Agnes a good life, and that the other chickens needed us too. But Pickle quieted me, and then she asked to be alone. My daughter was old enough to hold on to her sadness, and although I wanted badly to comfort her, I had to respect that.

37.

~~~

WHEN PICKLE WAS eleven years old, I sat on a park bench at the playground near the farmers market across the street from Cathlin's church and watched her and a friend take turns on a baby swing. They were much too big for the swing and had to force their long legs into the holes. They'd get stuck, then I'd have to walk over and dislodge them.

A small toddler watched the girls, his wordless wonder encapsulated in an outstretched pointer finger as if to say, "What gives? That's my swing!"

I suggested that Pickle and her friend move on to the tire swing so the little guy could have a chance. But the toddler followed them and looked eagerly at the big girls and their play. After asking his mother if it was okay, I lifted him onto the tire swing and gently pushed the three of them. Pickle gave the boy a pat and reassured him: "He's a good daddy," she said, which pleased me. But it also gave me a kind of emotional vertigo. In a manner of minutes, I traveled from Pickle's years in the baby swing, to the more mature tire swing, and now back to her actions as a compassionate eleven-year-old.

We moved to the Vineyard when Pickle was just a baby, much smaller than the toddler on the tire swing. The years slipped past faster, it seemed, than a lap around the playground. I've tried to keep my heart on pause with regard to Pickle growing up so quickly, but in the park, I felt it swell— and break a bit, too. I had bad news to tell Pickle and I had been stalling.

On the way to the park that day, I'd learned that the half-wild/half-tame rabbit that had come to be our pet, albeit a pet unlike any other, had died.

It's every parent's nightmare to have to tell their child about the death of a furry loved one. In this case, it was even more complicated, as the rabbit wasn't really ours. We often went weeks without seeing Alex, our name for the bunny, which also answered to Honey, Hey You, and Sir Hides a Lot, names other neighbors gave her (or him, as the sex was also debated within the neighborhood). Because of this, I could stall, and when Pickle eventually asked, I could offer something vague like, "Maybe Alex met a friend and moved on." It would be easy, I thought. But over the years, I had learned the words *easy* and *parenting* did not really go together.

ALEX HAD APPEARED suddenly in our lives about two years earlier, when she burst forth from under a rhododendron on the edge of our yard and ran toward us as we emerged from our car. "It must be rabid," I thought, this bunny racing to rather than away from us. But then it sat patiently, friendly and unafraid, at our feet while we scratched it behind the ears and petted its large hind legs.

Alex had the markings of a domestic rabbit, orange with white spots, unlike the pack of grayish brown bunnies that scattered when they saw us. And yet she survived out there in the woods, visiting us at random intervals. Once, a thoughtful neighbor caught the bunny and took it to the animal shelter, thinking it too tame to be wild, but unaware that it had several "owners" in the community.

"It's not Pickle's bunny, is it?" the neighbor asked me a few days later, when I inquired whether she had seen it.

"Not exactly . . . but sort of," I said, then drove to the shelter to retrieve Alex and set her free in the neighborhood once again.

When another neighbor conducted morning meetings in his driveway, giving his construction crew their assignments for the day, Alex sometimes sat at his feet like an assistant manager making sure the message was heard.

All of us in the neighborhood seemed to agree that there was something special about a pet that comes and goes and requires no work or cleanup. Each visit was magical because we never knew when Alex would arrive and how long she would stay.

Eventually, I discovered that the true owner lived not far from us. She told me Alex had been purchased at the pet store but kept picking the lock on the outdoor pen. When the lock was fortified, she tunneled under the fence to freedom, at which point the family decided to let her come and go at will.

A MONTH BEFORE Alex died, she hopped into our yard looking badly beat up. She had a scratch on her white nose, a bloody ear, and a gash along her throat. Her legs appeared fine, able to run toward us without a limp, and her spirits, if anything, seemed more affectionate than ever. She was also very thirsty.

I ran our outdoor shower until rivers of water appeared in the grass, which Alex lapped up for several minutes before getting her fill. Pickle plucked some choice clover and cut a carrot into small pieces. Alex ate out of our hands as we inspected her wounds. Her throat looked bad, a long scab already forming. She moved to a space beneath the porch where Pickle placed a bowl of water each morning before she left for school. I imagined Alex would be healthy again soon. But a few days later the cut on her neck worsened. Her constant scratching dug deeper into the skin until we could see bone protruding. While we debated bringing Alex to a veterinarian, she vanished.

The owner told me later that Alex had returned home to die. They took her to a vet who said there was no hope and put her to sleep to stop her suffering.

All this I knew and held tight against my chest, waiting for the right moment to tell Pickle.

A WEEK LATER, I still I hadn't told Pickle the news. But I began to think she knew, in the same way she knew the tooth fairy was really her delinquent dues-paying dad and that Santa was a construct she played along with to make me happy. Perhaps, like me, she was stalling to avoid the inevitably sad conversation we'd have.

That Saturday afternoon, I sat in my basement office reading a draft of Cathlin's sermon. It was about the trials of Job, the good and pious man who loses everything, his health, wealth, and family. It holds the foundation for theological discussions about why innocent people suffer or, rather, why no one is immune from suffering—it lurks around the corner for all of us, in large doses and small, from a young woman minister tending to her island flock while battling breast cancer to tame rabbits that have chosen to survive in the wild, to fathers trying to shield their little girls from bad news.

I put down the sermon and walked upstairs, where Pickle sat on the couch, pecking away at her computer. I thought she was watching a movie or playing a game and I was about to tell her enough screen time when she turned to me.

"Hey, Dad," she said, "will you read my story?"

"Of course," I said, and sat down next to her.

She placed the computer in my lap and I began reading. Her first sentence shocked me: her story was about Alex. She described the first time they met, and how she and a friend decided on the gender-neutral name Alex because they didn't know if it was a boy or a girl.

"Pickle," I asked, "do you want to know what happened to Alex?"

"I think I already do," she answered.

We talked on the couch for quite a while, about Alex and what she meant to us, and what her dying also meant to us. We talked about the gray in my beard and the new muscles in Pickle's arms. We talked about Hardy's shaving. We talked about Cathlin's breast cancer, so many years in the past but always present in the pills she took every day and the checkups with her oncologist. We talked about writing and how hard it is. We talked about time and how much a decade might weigh if you could find a scale big enough.

And we also talked about getting a puppy.

38.

~~~

I LIVE ON AN island crisscrossed with miles of wooded trails, but for years I rarely visited them. I live on an island ringed by beaches visible around almost every bend in the road, but for weeks at a time I would not see them—this was mostly an off-season lament, but sometimes even during summer my inland routines left me landlocked as though I had somehow settled down in Kansas or Oklahoma rather than a small island off the coast of Massachusetts.

All that changed after I finally gave in to Pickle's constant pleas for a dog.

My reasons for not wanting a dog were, I felt, valid. The children were workout enough, I told Cathlin, and what quiet time I could scratch out of a day, I didn't want to give back. For a long time, Pickle listened to my rebuttals to her appeals and would, after a little nagging, let the matter drop. But as my daughter grew older, her debating skills began to flourish.

"Can I have a dog?"

"No."

"Why not?"

"There are so many reasons."

Silence.

"Did you ever have a dog?"

"Yes."

"What was its name?"

"Triscuit."

"Did you love her?"

"Very much."

"Then why can't *I* have a dog to love?"

Pickle's offense was strong, and my best defense would have meant confessing something I was too ashamed to speak out loud. I had told my daughter that Triscuit died young, at three years old, and that I still felt the sting so many years later. But how to tell her that Triscuit died during wrestling season when I was a sophomore in high school, and because I didn't know how to express my grief, I didn't cry and instead took it out on a young boy from a neighboring high school? How to admit that I beat the boy more savagely than I needed to or had ever done before, while friends and teachers cheered me on from the stands because they couldn't hear the boy crying beneath me.

How to tell my young daughter all that? There was no way. So when Pickle was twelve, I gave in.

AT FIRST, I didn't like the new dog. My daughter named him Artichoke, a cute name for a cute puppy, but he didn't sleep, he needed to be walked early and late. The dog wanted my attention *all the time*, and I quickly became so frustrated and harried that I began lashing out: when Artichoke barked, I barked back; when Artichoke whined, I whined, too.

Pickle grew so worried about my behavior that one night at dinner, while I sat sulking, she said, "If you really think we need to, we can get rid of Artichoke . . . we can find him another home where people will love him . . . even the father." She was crying as she said it, but held her place at the table, trying to be strong.

There have been many moments of my parenting life that I'm ashamed of, but that scene quickly vaulted to high on the list. I vowed to do better.

Soon enough, something changed. Perhaps Artichoke became a little easier, bit by bit, as children do as they add years to their small selves, from toddler tantrums to kindergarten kindness to preteen wonders. I certainly know I became a better dog owner. It started the same way I became a better father, by letting go of my agenda and embracing the mysteries of my children's minds. It was a revelation then and it was again as I put aside my to-do lists to spend hours walking wooded trails and sandy beaches with Artichoke.

A summer friend introduced me to Lambert's Cove Beach, where a dog party raged each day until midmorning. I soon added a daily swim to my daily dog walk.

In the fall, the beach was open to dogs all day, but the crowd of owners and pets thinned. Some days Artichoke and I met no one on our walks, our summer friends dispersed to their winter homes, our island friends operating on different schedules. The gulls and the waves were the only constants.

One autumn day on the empty beach, after we'd had Artichoke for about a year, I watched him race ahead of me on the trail of a new and exciting scent. He was focused on what was ahead, but suddenly stopped and turned to look at me, as if to make sure I was nearby and still a part of his life. He cocked his furry head and his floppy ears perked up, and in that moment I recalled my children, soon after they had started walking, setting off to follow their curiosity, then stopping to look back and make sure I was close behind. My children no longer did this and I missed it deeply.

"I'm here," I called out to Artichoke.

He barked a reply and then disappeared around a bend, leaving me alone for a moment. And as the waves slowly lapped the shoreline and the wind picked up, I heard what I thought was a young boy crying in the distance—only this time it was me.

39.

ARRIVING IN PICKLE'S room one night to tuck her in, I found her with the covers up to her chin, her eyes wide and teary. Artichoke was at her feet, munching on his favorite purple stuffed animal.

"Why are you sad?" I asked, snugging her blankets around her.

"Because dogs don't live as long as humans," she answered. "And it's not fair that Artichoke will die and I'll have to watch."

Heavy stuff at bedtime, I thought.

"There's no point in thinking about this now," I told Pickle. "It's a long time in the future."

But at some point in my fatherly speech, it occurred to me that she might soon think the same thing about daughters and fathers, our future timetables also very unequal.

The weight of the thought drove me to my knees and then down onto my chest, where I started doing pushups, my talisman to ward off Father Time. When Pickle asked what I was doing, I blurted out, "Nothing . . ." But then Artichoke climbed on my back, so I told Pickle to climb aboard, too, and soon we were all laughing.

Later, I turned off Pickle's bedside light and she snuggled into her pillow, her face content for the moment. As for me, I knew sleep wouldn't come as easily.

40.

~~

I N THE EARLIEST days of the COVID-19 pandemic, when
the coronavirus still felt like something that was happening on the other side of the world, I learned about a Vineyard couple who were traveling on one of the cruise ships
that were denied port in Hong Kong, or anywhere else. After
weeks adrift, they were finally admitted to a port in Malaysia
and the couple began slowly making their way home. Once
they were back on the Vineyard, I had a reporter interview
them by phone as they quietly quarantined, and we told
their story in the *Gazette*.

At the *Gazette*, our mission is to focus our reporting on
the comings and goings of Martha's Vineyard. There are
plenty of good national papers for the national news, so we
stick to our shores. But since our shores are visited by people
from all over the world, we can often tap into stories that are
part of national and international stories.

The cruise ship couple's coronavirus odyssey gave us islanders our first glimpse of what would soon become the
pandemic. For a moment, we thought it was a story that
would remain "over there," on the far side of the globe. But
within a few weeks of publishing the couple's tale, we were

locked down like everyone else in the world. The *Gazette*'s coverage of what was happening on the Vineyard mirrored coverage elsewhere. Our story was everyone's story. And my story was everyone's story.

ON THE VINEYARD, we were used to not seeing many people in the off-season, of keeping to ourselves and not going out much, as most of the stores were closed in winter anyway. But as people decided to move to the island, summer people sheltering here or newcomers fleeing the cities, tempers occasionally flared. A freelance photographer at the *Gazette*, who mostly lived here full time but still had her Connecticut license plates, was often on the receiving end of nasty comments. She said she felt unsafe at times, so we varied her assignments, trying to gauge the risk level of both the pandemic and the community.

At home, Cathlin and I, like parents everywhere, tried to create some sense of normalcy and routine for the kids, even though we knew that nothing about the current situation was normal. One night several weeks in, while saying good-night to Pickle, I asked her if she wanted to walk, bike, or drive to school the next day.

"But I don't go to school anymore," she answered. This was before Zoom school had begun and teachers were sending lessons home by email.

"Today, at first-period home-school, you were a bit groggy," I said. "Let's mix it up, get some air first."

The next morning, after biking the one-mile loop around our neighborhood with full backpacks, we settled into a science lesson at the kitchen table. Pickle was doing a project on storms and had chosen tornadoes. She found a video on the internet by a weather-chaser called Pecos Bob that showed, in gruesome detail, his top ten tornadoes. It was both frightening and poetic.

As I tried to watch Pecos Bob's picks, Artichoke began barking, which was odd since no one came to the door anymore. I went to the window to check on what was causing the commotion and saw a neighbor wander by walking a goat.

Back in "the classroom," I tried to pivot between checking in with my boss and working on weekly weather statistics with Pickle. I fired off a quick text to my boss, some work stuff and bit of banter with her about not having enough caffeine that morning. Then I returned my attention to my daughter.

Ten or fifteen minutes later, I looked back at the text I'd sent and was horrified. I had spelled caffeine wrong and auto-correct inexplicably changed the word to Vagina Ted, as in: "I'm still groggy, I haven't had enough Vagina Ted this morning." I quickly texted my boss again, apologizing to her and adding that I definitely didn't know anyone by that name. She replied "No worries" and thanked me for the laugh.

Hardy, who was a sophomore in high school during the first winter of coronavirus, had hung a chart on his bedroom wall to mark off the days, like a prisoner looking ahead to his release. He had adjusted to quarantine life by watching movies, checking in with friends by text, and doing his homework all from the comfort of his bed. I would enter his room and push him from side to side, joking that I was a nurse making sure he didn't get bed sores, but I was only half joking.

On Sunday mornings, Cathlin held a virtual service for her congregation from the corner of our bedroom. She hung thick curtains on the window, a tapestry on the wall behind her, placed a few candles around the room. I would watch via Zoom from downstairs. In gallery mode, I could see the other congregants, including my mother and father. Cathlin led everyone in a welcoming prayer, then another person took center stage for a scripture reading, the music director played the piano from his living room, a member of the choir sang a solo from her dining room. It felt like church in many ways, except for one major difference: instead of being shoulder to shoulder in a pew, staring at the backs of each other's heads as we all faced forward to look at Cathlin, we looked at each other's faces.

One Sunday, Cathlin related a passage by Hildegard of Bingen, a twelfth-century Benedictine nun, mystic, and composer. Hildegard wrote that in order to achieve balance, we should fly with two wings of awareness: one of pain and suffering, the other of hope and beauty, because that's what life always brings. This made perfect sense to me amid the pandemic lockdown as each hour of the day seemed to leap from one emotion to another, from humor to pragmatic resolve to fear to sadness.

When Cathlin was going through chemotherapy for breast cancer but still leading services most weeks, she woke one Sunday morning and found her hair had fallen out. It was more sudden than we expected, but only because in those days we never knew what to expect. A neighbor shaved Cathlin's head to even out the clumps and an hour later she preached a sermon about delivering herself into a fire of love in order to come out the other side forever changed and somehow stronger than before. I wept that day in church as I listened to my brave wife. Sitting alone in my kitchen in front of my computer screen, absorbing Cathlin's sermon about Hildegard's two wings of awareness, was only the second time I ever cried in church. I turned off my computer so I didn't have to watch myself, but the tears felt helpful, as they always do.

ONE EVENING I made a plan with Hardy to watch a movie together, just the two of us. Pickle was not happy with this and kept asking why she couldn't be part of the plan. I spent so much of each day with Pickle, the needs of an extroverted twelve-year-old sometimes subsuming the household, but I knew fifteen-year-old Hardy needed me, too, even if he wasn't vocal about it. I got frustrated with Pickle's whining and snapped at her. She stormed outside, taking a book, blanket, and pillow with her. I watched from the window, impressed as she climbed onto the roof of the car and built a reading nook there, complete with raised hatchback for a back rest.

Then Hardy and I retreated to the basement to watch *The Deer Hunter*.

We had often talked about watching the movie together but could never find the time for the three-hour epic. Now we had nothing but time. The first hour was as gorgeous as I remembered, depicting a small Pennsylvania town and a group of friends about to head off to Vietnam. But then in the second hour the friends go to war, and the darkness and horror was almost too much for me. I looked over at Hardy. He was rapt and so we continued, and I was glad we did. As a family we'd been watching a steady diet of Wes Anderson movies, enjoying his absurdist escapism, but *The Deer Hunter* helped me access a wider range of emotions.

I continued to peek at Hardy and realized he was exactly the same age I was when I first saw the movie. When I was fifteen, I spent the summer at wrestling camp in western New Jersey, where a new friend named Danny led a skit about the movie, somehow turning the darkest scenes into humor-filled parodies. I knew Danny only that one summer, living together for five weeks as campers and counselors. A few years later I heard from friends that Danny was killed while trying to stop a fight, the good Samaritan tale gone horribly wrong. But there in my basement with Hardy, I could see Danny's smile again, along with the smiles of so many others. During lockdown, I found I spent a lot of time in my mind with people who had brought me joy, who knew me as a boy, a teenager, a college kid, a young man, a gray-haired father. Others were doing the same thing, I discovered, as I received as many texts and emails from the past as I sent out.

Later that night, after everyone else was in bed, I sat down at my computer to check on the world one last time before turning in. I found a small blue notecard on my desk with Pickle's handwriting. She often did this, left notes for me to find. Usually, they were scraps of good cheer to lift me up after a hard day.

This was not one of those notes.

"Dear Dad," she wrote. "I am sorry that I annoy you with questions. I will try to be less curious and remember things better. Tell me whatever I can do to make these days better for you. I love you. Pickle."

I collapsed on the floor, then picked myself up and walked upstairs to her room. Pickle was asleep but I crawled into bed with her and hugged her tightly. She stirred and I whispered how much I loved her and that I wanted her never to stop being curious.

Then I lay there, long into the night, waving to all the people I'd traveled with during this lifetime and watched them wave back at me, all of us struggling to fly on wings heavy with hope and sorrow.

41.

W E WERE ALL asleep by eleven o'clock. Three hours later, our alarms rousted us from our beds. It was peak viewing time for the Lyrid meteor shower. If daytime during the pandemic offered little variety after being sheltered in place for more than a month, at least nighttime promised a show.

The dog was especially confused as we all made our way to the backyard. The cold air hit us as we wrapped ourselves in blankets, climbed onto the trampoline, and lay down together to look up at the clear night sky. It felt like a cross between fishing and fireworks: we waited and waited for that slight tug on the line, and then, as if out of nowhere, from the deep, endless pool of space, a star would flash across the sky. There were small streaks, medium streaks, and bold flashes. We all cheered quietly, our faces tilted upward, smiling at the heavens.

I was the first to leave, slipping away saying I was cold and wanted the warmth of my bed.

Inside, I walked up the steps to the second floor and opened the window that looks out on our backyard. I heard the indiscernible mumble of my wife and children's chatter and their exclamations of awe. I heard the wind and small creatures scuttling about in the dark. I heard from my younger self and my future self, too. I heard from friends and family, ghosts of the living and the dead. I heard my heart thumping and a world crying. All this I heard one night while watching my family watch the stars.

42.

⁓⁓⁓

"DAD," SAID PICKLE, "tell me about the old days . . . when life was normal and we could go out and do things, like play with friends and drive off-island for adventures."

We were near the end of our nighttime routine. The dog was curled up next to Pickle on the pillow, his eyes half-mast, getting ready to dream about his girlfriend, the dog next door.

I smiled and said, "Okay." These end-of-the-day moments were familiar and comforting. Before the pandemic I often I rushed through them, but now we had nothing but time.

I lay down next to Pickle, looked up at the ceiling, and thought for a moment.

"What do you want to hear?" I asked.

"How about that time we were surrounded by a busload of drunk Canadian women who wanted to take you home, back across the border," Pickle suggested.

"Oh, one of my favorites," I responded, and we settled in.

It was Pickle's tenth birthday and to celebrate I took her to see a Taylor Swift show in Boston, her first concert and my first tween show. It was high summer and the world was full of activity back then—beaches crowded, shops bustling, and music filling the air. The memory seemed almost incomprehensible now—flashes of tailgating and walking with thousands of other fans into Gillette Stadium—which is why Pickle and I kept telling these stories to each other, to take us back to the world we once knew.

"Remember how long the ice cream line was?" I asked Pickle.

It was filled with moms and daughters and nearly ten times as long as the beer and wine line. This was definitely not Dadland, but I took it in stride, waving and laughing at Pickle stuck in the ice-cream line as I made it through the beer line with ease.

When we found our seats, a party was already in full swing. Pickle and I were an island of two surrounded by twenty Canadian women ranging in age from thirty to sixty and a sober bus driver in her seventies. None of them had brought kids.

It didn't take long for us to become fast friends. The women had traveled from a small town outside of Toronto. They planned to do a bit of sightseeing in Boston, too, but today was all about Taylor Swift. One woman, Daphne, told me she had left her daughter at home with her no-good ex-husband.

"I think Daphne kind of liked you," Pickle said, interrupting my story.

Yes, I thought, it certainly looked that way, when Daphne peered deeply into my eyes as if trying to magnetize my soul and take it with her.

"Pickle," I said, "do you remember what I told you that day? She only liked the *idea* of me."

"What does that mean again?"

"Well, a guy being nice to his kid in public has it made. As long as he doesn't lose his temper and mostly stays off his phone, he's treated like a king. It's been that way for me since you were born. Once, when I was pushing you in a stroller, a woman stopped her car, rolled down the window, and growled at me."

"That's *weird*," Pickle said. "Does that happen to Mom, too?"

"She's never mentioned it," I replied.

Pickle chewed on this thought silently for a moment and then took us back to the past. "Remember when you left me alone at the concert because you had to go to the bathroom?"

"You weren't alone," I said. "You were with your new Canadian aunties."

When I needed to use the restroom, Pickle didn't want to leave our seats, so when our new friends offered to watch her, I was grateful.

But when I returned, Pickle was gone.

"Oh, she went with Daphne to get some more beer and ice cream," one of the women told me.

I froze and imagined the newspaper headlines: *Idiot Dad Loses Daughter at Taylor Swift Show.*

After what felt like an unbearably long time, they returned, with Pickle leading the way.

"Daphne got kind of lost and confused out there in the beer line," Pickle told me. "But I found our way back."

Ah, I told myself as my racing heart began to slow, *I'm teaching independence and survival skills.*

The concert started and was an incredible three-hour sing-along and dance marathon with our new friends. I knew most of the songs, though not every word like everyone else at the show. But it didn't matter. Our seatmates filled in the gaps. And when my feet started to hurt, Daphne danced with Pickle deep into the night.

When the show ended, our group sat together, lingering and enjoying our newfound friendship, strangers brought together in a shared experience. We all hugged and took photographs, which came out mostly blurry, unlike the crystal-clear memory.

"That's how it was in the old days," I said to Pickle, as we rested shoulder to shoulder on her bed.

It was late, past Pickle's bedtime, but we turned on some Taylor Swift and listened as she sang to us that *everything will be alright if we just keep dancing like we're twenty-two.*

"Do you think it will ever be like that again?" Pickle whispered.

"Definitely," I said. "Daphne would demand it."

43.

~~~~~

As the weather warmed after that first winter of COVID-19 lockdown, I gave myself a crew cut. I didn't know how long it would be before I could visit a barber and figured I might as well do it myself, so I took my electric clippers into the backyard. It didn't take long, a few passes around my head as the hair piled up on the grass. Afterward, I gathered the clumps and placed them at the edge of the yard near the bird feeder as an offering of nesting material.

It felt good to rub my hand on my nubby scalp. As a boy, I liked to get crew cuts during wrestling season; they made me feel tough and focused. My new crew cut helped me feel that way again, which was good, because on so many days during the pandemic I wanted to crawl under the bed and hide.

But my new look was not without its downsides. Pickle cried out in shock, telling me I looked old and bald. Hardy told me my ears were massive and that I looked like an elf. I also felt a bit sad because I had shaved off a special haircut, one I gotten just before the pandemic started. That appointment had been one I enjoyed once a year, every year, for a decade.

BEFORE CHEMOTHERAPY MADE Cathlin's hair fall out, her team at the hospital had sent us to The Salon at 10 Newbury where we met the owner and wigmaker extraordinaire, Patricia Wrixon.

The first time we visited the salon, Patricia met us at the front desk and led us past the rows of busy stylists. I cried often in those days, sometimes quietly, sniffling to myself, and other times explosively, the full force of what our lives had become catching me unaware like a sneeze. Sitting with Patricia and Cathlin, talking about wigs and baldness, was one of the times I lost it. Excusing myself, I dashed from the room, planning to walk the streets until my tears subsided.

But as I walked past the rows of people taking part in a normal Friday ritual of getting ready for the weekend and nights out, I saw a man standing beside his empty stylist's chair. He smiled and motioned me to sit. Without thinking, I did.

We introduced ourselves. His name was Elie Ferzli. We barely spoke as he cut and I wept. He didn't charge me.

A few weeks later, Cathlin's hair fell out. We thought it would be gradual, giving us time to adapt, but cancer, we learned, wasn't orderly—it was chaos of a different kind, filled with confusion and too much time to think about worst-case scenarios. I tried to beat back the fear by doing a lot of pushups outside in the dark of night. Something about gripping the cold earth with my hands felt comforting. Chemotherapy was followed by a double mastectomy and then months of radiation. And then, finally, a cancer-free diagnosis.

AT FIRST, CATHLIN returned to Boston twice a year for checkups. Satisfied with her progress, her doctors eventually moved her to annual visits, which she continues to this day. The trips no longer filled us with dread, at least not the heavy type that turned a normally busy and loud family into a quiet one where even our children would press PAUSE on their exuberance as they waited for their mother to return from Mass General with news. Now, so many years and checkups later, it's merely part of our routine.

Cathlin kept in touch with the cancer team, who became our friends. While she has her oncologist and the nursing staff as reminders of the positive side of those dark days, I have my annual visit to Newbury Street, where I return to sit at Elie Ferzli's station.

Though we saw each other just once a year, for less than an hour each visit, and didn't correspond, after a decade I came to count Elie as a dear friend; I believe he felt the same way about me.

Every time I returned to sit in Elie's chair, we checked in with each other, which, for the first few years, meant Elie asking me how Cathlin was doing. Then one year, when I called for my annual appointment, the receptionist told me Elie would be out for several months. She couldn't tell me why.

A year later, when I returned to his salon chair, Elie told me he had been diagnosed with multiple myeloma, a cancer of the bone marrow. After chemotherapy and stem cell treatments, he had to protect his immune system by staying in isolation for four months, unable to walk the streets or even hug his wife or son. Looking at him behind me in the mirror as he told me this, I was stunned. He was healthy again, bent over my hair and moving about with ease. Around us, customers and their stylists carried on their own conversations, the hum of voices mixing with the sounds of scissors and blow dryers.

THE YEARS PILED up. Our children grew. Elie and I shifted from conversations about preschool to talks of grammar school to conversation about high school. We grew beards and shaved them off. My hair began to thin, and I worried about going bald, partly out of vanity but also fear of not needing my annual visit with Elie.

I brought Cathlin to meet him, and then the children. When he met Pickle, Elie held out his hand and said, "Nice to meet you, I'm Cucumber."

In February, a month before the COVID-19 lockdown, I sat down in his chair and asked him about his health, and if he was still feeling fine. He replied, "Well, let's define *fine*."

Elie told me his cancer had returned, but the doctors were keeping it at bay with twice-a-week chemo.

I looked at him, incredulous. He seemed as energetic as ever. "How are you still working?" I asked. "When Cathlin had chemo, she'd lie in bed for days."

"I don't feel the effects," he said. "Never have. After treatments, I go play volleyball."

Elie kept talking and cutting that cold February day, telling me about the particulars of his disease, which would remain in his body until new drugs were discovered. He could only receive one more bone marrow transplant, but the doctors were saving that heavy-duty treatment for later. For the time being, it would be chemo and volleyball.

"Enough about this," he said. "Let's make your hair smile."

Then we fell silent. And as I listened to the gentle snip of his scissors and watched his reflection in the mirror, I thought of how Cathlin had her oncology team and I had Elie to remind me of the cancer days, both the bad and the good. Pushing Cathlin in a wheelchair through the hospital when she was bald and pale and weak, people turned their heads, and I could almost hear them thinking, "There goes someone in worse shape than me." It was a time filled with fear and uncertainty, but it was a golden time, too, when trivialities evaporated leaving behind only love.

Sitting in his chair that day, I grew worried about Elie. For the first time in our long relationship, I asked him for his phone number so we could keep in touch more often.

AFTER THE PANDEMIC hit, I wanted to call Elie to check in, but I kept stalling. I feared for his health and knew I couldn't take any more bad news. But eventually I did call, and he answered right away. He reassured me that he was fine and able to still have his chemo through a separate hospital entrance, but no more volleyball, as the gym had closed down.

We talked a little longer, and I told him about my self-administered, backyard crew cut.

"I bet you look handsome," he said.

I didn't, but it was nice to hear.

44.

~~~

THE SUMMER PICKLE was three years old and the Reverend Raphael Warnock came for his annual visit to Martha's Vineyard, she grabbed him by the hand and led him upstairs to her room to give him a tour of her extensive dead-bug collection.

Nine years later we found ourselves in the living room of Raphael's home in Atlanta while he explained that his son, who was two years old at the time, had a dead-bug collection of his own, although his was more specific.

"Lady bugs," Raphael said with a laugh. "He collects dead lady bugs."

But Pickle wasn't there to compare dead-bug collections. She was there, as we all were, to canvass for Raphael.

In November 2020, neither Raphael nor his Republican opponent had won a majority of the vote in the special election for U.S. Senate, so a runoff was being held on January 5, 2021. The day after Christmas, after Cathlin had finished the journey of advent, preaching by Zoom to her congregation, we'd packed up the family, including Artichoke, and driven to Georgia to poster the streets and beat the pavement going door to door to get out the vote for Raphael's historic bid to represent Georgia. The state hadn't elected a Democrat since 2000, and had never elected a Black senator.

On New Year's Eve, the special election was five days away. That night, after knocking on doors all day to get out the vote, we celebrated quietly at our Airbnb with Raphael and his sister. The windows were open, we were masked and social distanced, but we were together.

Raphael told us stories about the campaign trail, about all the people he had met across Georgia, about hiring a staff and learning the ways of campaigning (his first), and the origins of his puppy commercials, which went viral.

In turn, we told him about watching election volunteer-training videos every evening and then being deployed around the city during the day, helping to counter voter suppression.

Many of the neighborhoods we visited had fallen on hard times, disenfranchised places where people struggled in ways we could only imagine. In a former life, I would have avoided the neighborhoods, but on that trip, I took my children there and felt a sense of pride as I watched sixteen-year-old Hardy walk up to a stranger's door to encourage him to vote. But my bubble quickly popped when a hard-looking young man answered the door and told Hardy, "Get the fuck off my porch!" We beat a hasty retreat.

That's what the ground game looked like. Moments of anger or knocking for nothing—no one home yet again— offset by moments of beauty, such as when a woman came to the door and we explained that her absentee ballot had been rejected and she needed to return to her voting station to fix it. She put her hands together in prayer and thanked us.

At one house, Pickle and I knocked on a door and then stepped back to create social distance while we waited for a response. But when I did, I heard something metallic at our feet. I looked down and saw that I had kicked a bullet shell casing. I looked around and noticed that the front yard was littered with various types of casings, different sizes, shapes, and colors. Pickle and I backed away and moved on to the next house.

When Pickle told Raphael this story at the end of the day, he suggested we come to Savannah for the weekend. He was holding a rally there, his hometown, with Vice President-elect Kamala Harris, among others.

RAPHAEL'S VIRAL CAMPAIGN commercials showed how much he loved dogs and they loved him. But while we were in Georgia, I wasn't exactly loving our dog.

We brought Artichoke along with us to Savannah—when we travel as a family, we leave no one behind—but soon found out that dogs couldn't attend rallies. The event was scheduled to be four hours long and so I did the dad thing, taking it for the team and driving with Artichoke back to Atlanta.

Later that night, texts from the kids rolled in.

"Dad, after the rally we went out with Raphael to a restaurant."

"Dad, people keep coming up to the table. Raphael just took pictures with two little boys."

"Dad, the owner of the restaurant stopped by to say hello. She was at home but ran down the street when she heard Raphael was here. She told him her family is all Republican, but she's for Raphael."

"Dad, we got to see inside Raphael's campaign bus."

"Dad, we wish you were here with us."

THE NEXT DAY, back together in Atlanta, we hit the campaign trail again, driving, walking, talking, calling, doing whatever our ever-growing network of staffers and volunteers asked us to do. The organization was incredible.

On January 4, I walked the streets and saw signs and posters and images of Raphael. I swung from excitement to anxiety every few minutes. We all did. We couldn't sleep. We stress-ate. We watched the movie *Selma*.

We attended a rally with President-elect Joe Biden. We stood in the front row and watched our friend Raphael with Biden, and listened to the crowd of thousands erupt. We cheered along with them. Pickle and I even invented a little dance routine and a man said to me, "Nice moves!" I had never in my life been told I had nice moves, but there in Atlanta, anything felt possible.

ON ELECTION DAY we all woke at 5:30 a.m. to start the day as poll monitors. Cathlin put on her white clerical collar and I marveled, as I so often did, at this woman I've known since we were in high school. She has always walked the heartfelt path, the way of humility and justice and selfless courage. For so long, I felt as if I walked with her from a bit of a distance where activism and standing up for what you believe was concerned, not wanting or knowing how to put myself on the line. But on that morning in Georgia, I was side by side with my wife.

At our polling location, many voters were distressed to discover they were at the wrong one. We gave them directions to their correct polling location, urging them to stay the course and get their vote counted. Every potential voter seemed focused and determined, and I let myself begin to believe—just a little bit.

In the afternoon, we knocked on more doors. I met a woman who attended Raphael's church and she told me she remembered Cathlin preaching at Ebenezer Baptist Church, remembered her words and her spirit. We were masked but there was no stopping our hug.

In the evening, we drove to a place called the Georgia Beer Garden, across from Warnock campaign headquarters. A few friends and family gathered there to watch the returns with Raphael. People kept texting me. Their energy was frenetic. But in the bar, it was mellow. Raphael chatted quietly with everyone, didn't even glance at the TV, and acknowledged it would be a long night or, more likely, several days before the results would be known.

But as the evening wore on, the mood shifted: up, down, up, down and then up, up, up. Raphael and his team moved across the street, back to their headquarters, to prepare. Then we were told to come across the street, too, to be part of the historic moment. We walked through a metal detector and upstairs to the campaign war room.

When the verdict was clear, the campaign manager whispering the numbers coming in from DeKalb County, a few moments before NBC's Steve Kornacki would deliver them nationally, a ripple moved through those of us gathered in the small room. It started quietly, almost tentatively, but then exploded with cheers and clapping and tears.

Before making a speech, before giving thanks, Raphael called his eighty-two-year-old mother in Savannah.

"Mom, can you hear me?" he asked. "This is Reverend Senator Warnock calling."

The crowd erupted again in cheers and then quieted down as Raphael listened to his mother on the phone. He turned to everyone.

"She says she's still just *Mama*."

THE DAY AFTER the election I got up before dawn. We were up late celebrating, but I couldn't sleep. I drove to Chrome Yellow, the coffee shop I had visited every morning while in Atlanta to start my day. After I got coffee and walked to my car, I suddenly didn't feel like driving straight back to the house, so I started wandering.

Atlanta is a city of murals. I walked down Edgewood Avenue and past a mural of the late congressman John Lewis. A few more steps and I passed a mural of Stacey Abrams. Then George Floyd appeared, three stories high. I turned off Edgewood and down Jackson, which led to Ebenezer Baptist Church and the Martin Luther King Jr. Center for Nonviolent Social Change. All along the way were images of Raphael Warnock. My heart was so full that I decided to keep walking.

On the campaign trail, Raphael often told a story about his father, who used to wake him at six in the morning and say, "Put your shoes on, son. Get ready. There's something for you to do."

The sun was rising in Atlanta. I had my shoes on. And I was ready.

45.

WE ARRIVED BACK on Martha's Vineyard to find it blanketed in snow. Shoveling, I paused to rest, breathing deeply. I gazed into the woods and noticed a rhododendron, its buds small and closed and dusted white. And with that I was off, thousands of miles away and decades earlier, to a time when I wore a younger man's muscles. Proust had his madeleines; I have this island.

The rhododendron I'd seen so long ago was impossibly tall and blooming a deep red. It was part of a full forest by the side of a mountain trail in Nepal that I had been walking for a month. The altitude was high and the air thin, but I wouldn't lessen my stride. In my twenties, I had no idea where I was headed but ran everywhere at full speed. It was a time when nothing seemed to make sense and yet everything was always in bloom.

As I leaned on the shovel, watching my breath smoke through the air, I wondered what in the future might cause me to remember this seemingly mundane afternoon. I looked all around me. The world was white, tree branches dipped to the ground under the weight of the snow, and dusk settled in. Inside the house, my family sat by the fire, waiting for me. And, all at once, I was stunned by how remarkable the moment was—and that I would never forget it.

46.

≈≈

IT WAS A cold, clear day and Hardy was driving me around
the island, from Oak Bluffs to Edgartown, across to Vineyard Haven, then up through West Tisbury, Chilmark, and
Aquinnah. Hardy was sixteen now and as the pandemic
eased and some normalcy returned, he began taking the
required driver's ed course. I would drop him off at school
and watch him drive away, a stranger in the passenger seat
helping him learn the ropes. But Hardy needed a lot of hours
behind the wheel to prepare for his driver's test, so on weekends I became his copilot, trying not to offer too much advice and mostly succeeding. We didn't have a set route; the
journey was one of feel and finding more roads to travel on
this small island.

From the passenger seat, I only occasionally resorted to
stomping the floor at an imaginary brake, when he rounded a turn too fast or an approaching car felt menacing. But
then again, everything feels scary when you're relegated to
the passenger seat of your son's life. I glanced at him, this
young man with two strong hands on the wheel, a bit of
stubble on his chin, his profile steady as he looked ahead
down the road.

Sometimes we talked on these drives, sometimes we remained silent or listened to the radio. On this wintery afternoon, we were quiet and my thoughts wandered as I looked out at the ocean view beyond South Road. When Hardy was born, I chose to step away from the working world to be a stay-at-home dad. This was not an easy fit at first and many days I took the difficulty of parenting personally. But eventually I learned that it's hard for everyone—for moms, dads, anyone trying to raise a child, either at home in the trenches or at work. Years later, I realized that one of the toughest things to digest as parents was that our former selves were immediately and abruptly erased as we navigated this new life of guiding and protecting our children. But it was also a beautiful ride. And it went by too fast.

As we rounded the Gay Head Cliffs, where I took Hardy as a young boy to prowl the shoreline tucked between the pounding ocean and the immense clay cliffs, my mind drifted further back to another time in a passenger seat, riding shotgun in Florida in a pickup truck being driven to a fishing hole by one of my graduate school professors, Bob Shacochis. The night before, Bob had thrown a party at his house and the next morning we were rolling ice cold cans of RC Cola across our foreheads to ease the pain of our hangovers. Half-eaten Arby's breakfast sandwiches sat in our laps.

The week before, Bob had torn apart one of my essays during our classroom workshop, going to great lengths to describe its sorry state, its lack of heart, its falseness. In the truck, I decided to take advantage of our time alone together, to try and go a bit deeper than class time allowed.

"What do you think is my biggest impediment to becoming a good writer?" I asked, as I nibbled at my egg sandwich.

"Using the word *impediment* is a start," Bob said. "That, and being earnest."

When I asked him to elaborate, he grunted. "You have to figure that out . . ."

Near the end of that semester, Hardy was born. I had another essay due and, as a new father, very little time to write. Cathlin and I were up every night with Hardy, a horrible sleeper of Herculean proportions. Out of desperation for something to write about, I turned to what was directly in front of me: hours-long stroller walks through the streets of Tallahassee, just me and my son taking the day more by whimper than by storm.

Bob praised the essay and told me I was close, very close. I was pleased by his encouragement but also afraid, because for the first time I had revealed something so quiet and personal.

As Hardy and I cruised down-island, we passed the Tashmoo overlook, where I'd recently taken Pickle and her friends sledding. They were all on the cusp of being teenagers, but on that day they'd giggled and frolicked like children.

We continued onward and I looked out at the Little League field where for so many years each spring our lives were swallowed up entirely and delightfully with Hardy playing and me coaching. But instead of remembering baseball heroics, my mind drifted back to Florida again, to the time I accompanied Cathlin on a business trip to Orlando. We were still living in New York City then and I was a full-time stay-at-home dad. My life had grown small, I thought, structured around naps, feedings, and trips to the park with

Hardy. I jumped at the chance to go on the business trip just to alter the sameness of every day.

The first morning in Orlando, up early with Hardy, I checked out the hotel dining room and buffet, lingering as long as I could with Hardy to give Cathlin more time to sleep and prepare for a meeting. Hotel guests scurried about, and as I waited in line for a cup of coffee, I turned to a woman standing behind me. My life at that time was moms and nannies, playgroups and burp cloths, so without thinking I brought this stranger into my stereotype.

"Is your husband here for a convention?" I asked her.

The woman looked at me with a confused expression.

"My husband is at home," she said. "I'm at a convention."

"Oh," I said, trying to recover. "Which one?"

"Women in aviation," she said. "I fly jets."

After a pause, she asked, "And what do *you* do?"

"I'm a stay-at-home dad."

Over the next three days, I saw this woman everywhere, but every time after our awkward meeting in the line for coffee she was dressed in her flight suit, surrounded by more women in cool-looking jump suits. We would wave to each other and once she came over to say hello, to pat Hardy on the head and wish us a good day sightseeing.

Whenever I retell this story, I play it mostly for laughs: my idiotic assumption and the woman's *Top Gun* comeback. But the story also stung a bit as I remembered that period, when I felt removed from my own life's desires. But on the drive, when I looked over at Hardy confidently gripping the steering wheel, I could also see other details from that trip: the many adult-sized Goofys and Donald Ducks wandering about that made Hardy laugh or cry depending on their proximity, teaching my son baby sign language so we could communicate long before he could talk, and my wife bent over her notes as she prepared to shine.

HARDY NAVIGATED FIVE Corners, using the hand-over-hand technique his driving instructor had taught him, and as I watched, I noticed the scar on his index finger. My children have always loved my scars, seeing each one as a chapter in a storybook. When they were younger, Hardy and Pickle would point to my thigh and ask me to tell them again about the moped accident, or at my chin and the time Uncle Jim dropped me when I was little. And, of course, as they grew they gathered their own scars and stories.

When Hardy was six or seven, we made our daily stop at the post office. He loved to turn the key in the box and behold its mysterious contents, the envelopes and magazines, occasional package, and on Fridays the *Vineyard Gazette*. I unstrapped him from his car seat and stepped back to let him climb out of the car. But in his excitement, he slammed the car door shut on his finger. I can still hear his scream. I ran to the door, opened it, and looked down at his mangled little finger. Somehow, I managed to get him back in his car seat and began driving to the hospital.

As we drove, Hardy screamed. In between gulping breaths he accused me of slamming the door on his finger. In my fear and racing adrenaline I went into defense mode and instead of consoling my son, I yelled at him. I told him it was all his fault and that I was not to blame.

The memory of my reaction hurts even more than the memory of his mangled finger.

OUR TRIP AROUND the island came to a close as Hardy steered the car into our driveway. For a moment I flashed back to Florida and my professor: We were on the wide-open Gulf reeling in fish as he told me stories about how he became a writer, the winding road from his childhood growing up outside of Washington, D.C., to his first book, and I listened intently. Then I was propelled forward in time, to years later when I sent Bob an essay I'd written while watching my children closely, trying to make sense of my life by capturing the details of theirs. Over time, I had come to realize what he wanted for me and for my writing: He wanted me to feel fully—from the hurt to the healing—but he also wanted me to be careful to not fall into the trap of earnestness by reporting only the good news. But there was no worry about that.

"With parenting," I wrote him, "you often end up being both the villain and the hero many times in the course of a single day. My children taught me that."

"That's it," he wrote back. " That's exactly it."

Hardy parked and turned off the car.

"How did I do, Dad?" he asked.

"You did great," I said. "But maybe go a bit slower next time."

47.

~~~

W HEN HARDY WAS seventeen and a senior in high
school, we drove south together on I-95 for his first
college tour. He was already taller than me and had been
shaving for years, but his deep voice still surprised me. He
was a young man, but when I glanced at him in the passenger seat, I could still see the baby he'd once been—sort of.

I had heard the college tours could be beautiful bonding experiences, that the long drives with the future firmly
planted center stage were ripe for talks about life and growth
and the passing down of generational knowledge. But the
only thing I could think about as we traveled along the highway was my funeral.

"How about the Vangelis score from *Chariots of Fire*," I
suggested, referring to the stirring music to one of my favorite movies. Hardy and I first watched it together at three in
the morning when he was about eight years old. I couldn't
sleep and was up late watching TV. Hardy couldn't sleep either—he could never sleep as a little kid—and he had joined
me on the couch. He seemed to like the slow-moving story
about four U.K. runners preparing for the 1924 Olympics,
which surprised me.

"Opening or closing?" Hardy asked.

"What?"

"Do you want the music to play at the beginning of your funeral service or the end?" he clarified.

"Oh, the beginning, definitely," I said. "That way everyone will be imagining youth and potential glory. That sort of thing."

"Got it," Hardy said, and pretended to jot it down in an imaginary notebook.

I wasn't sick and so these funeral arrangements weren't pressing. But it was a long drive and I couldn't help where my mind traveled. Hardy wanted to drive but I wouldn't let him. He was a good driver and had highway experience but something about the trip made me want to sit in the driver's seat. It was an illusion of course, that I was still in control of the direction his life would take, but I couldn't help myself.

After some more song selections for my funeral had been made, Hardy began updating me on the current horrors of the world. He had become a news hound and frequently re-cited events and statistics about the terrible realities of the human condition.

This was how we rolled along: making funeral arrange-ments for me while also growing somewhat depressed about the sorry state of the world. And as we continued down the road, I thought about how much I would miss it.

I HAD BEEN excited to show Hardy around my alma mater. But as we parked and got ready to the take the official tour, I suddenly felt like we could be at Anywhere University. As I tried to see it through my son's eyes, I couldn't connect. The past had been swallowed by the future. I walked mutely through the tour listening to anecdotes from the guide but mostly distracted as I thought about all the things I hadn't yet taught my son—the fade-away jumper, how to drive a stick shift. During Cathlin's pregnancy with Hardy, I became obsessed with all of my loose change, desperate to gather my pennies and dimes into rolls. If I could just coordinate my change before he was born, I thought, I'd be ready for fatherhood. As I half-listened to the campus tour guide, I thought: *If only I can teach my son to throw a tight spiral, I'll be ready for him to leave me.*

The guide said something funny and everyone laughed, but I drifted back to the delivery room and then home from the hospital, trying to figure out with Cathlin the enormity of what we didn't know about raising a child, which was basically everything, including how to keep him alive.

Hardy was born with a muscular condition in his neck called torticollis, a long word that basically means there was an injury to his neck in utero and he had trouble moving his head. But it wasn't obvious at first. Neither Cathlin nor I noticed it, just like we didn't notice he wasn't nursing properly because he couldn't latch on to Cathlin's breast and take in milk. We only noticed that he cried a lot and seemed to be getting thinner.

We were living in Florida, far away from family and friends who could have passed down information and lessons, who could have told us our child was starving. I have photographs of those early days, as all parents do, but it's hard to look at them, stills of Hardy struggling desperately to tell us he needed help. In one photo, his little hand is raised in a fist as he lies back on the bed wearing only a diaper—the power symbol is offset by his scowl and bony ribs.

Eventually, Cathlin and I discovered what was wrong and learned how to feed our son. But the memory of those days and our ignorance haunts me still.

AFTER THE TOUR, Hardy and I looked for a place to eat. We settled in at a small restaurant but instead of talking to my son about his future, all I wanted to talk about was our past together.

Soon after Hardy was born, I became obsessed with baby sign language, something I had read about in one of the many parenting books I'd devoured. We started when he was about seven months old, when, according to the books, a baby's mind is capable of communication but the physical elements of verbal language are still many months away. I wasn't satisfied with the few elementary signs I saw some of the other babies using down at the playground, banging their small fists together to ask for more or making a small circle with their thumb and forefinger to ask for a Cheerio.

I started by flapping my arms every time I saw a bird and eventually Hardy caught on, moving his arms up and down whenever a pigeon flew by. We'd left Florida by then and returned to New York City, so this was a constant occurrence. Then we moved on to more animals (bear, chicken, gorilla, elephant), verbs, and eventually the near equivalent of sentences: *I want* (pat the chest) *to go outside* (turn an imaginary doorknob) *to see the squirrels* (pretend to nibble an acorn). Soon, we were like a couple of third-base coaches flashing our signs to communicate even when standing far away from each other.

Hardy had heard the baby sign language story many times, but as I told it again over dinner, I understood more fully that he had no actual memory of those moments—it was all secondhand knowledge, an "as told-to-him" memory. It struck me that this was the way it would be for me the following year after he'd gone off to college: I'd learn about his life through phone calls and visits home rather than being there in the moment.

After dinner, I suggested we take a walk.

I showed Hardy a few of my old dorms, pointing to windows I once looked out from while wondering where my life would take me. We wandered until it was time to drop him off with an undergraduate wrestler I knew from helping him study for his SATs, who was taking Hardy that night to show him what college was like outside of the classroom. The three of us talked for a bit, but I quickly felt like a third wheel.

"Don't go crazy," I said to Hardy.

I turned and walked quickly out of sight, looking for a place to sit and collect myself. I saw another mom and daughter I'd met briefly on the tour. We smiled and waved but didn't talk, as they were enclosed in their own bubble.

I sat there on my own and thought back to Hardy and our sign-language days and to next fall when Cathlin and I would drop him off at college. I could see it, that leaving moment, when he had turned away and I was standing there wondering what to do with my hands. I would shout to him, I decided, hoping desperately that he would turn around so I could flash every sign I knew to tell him how much I loved him.

48.

A FELLOW FATHER CALLED to say he wasn't doing well. A stay-at-home dad with two kids under five years old, he was feeling swallowed up. His feelings went far beyond just exhaustion. He didn't say as much, but I knew what he meant. Hardy and Pickle were seventeen and fourteen years old, and I had been back at work for over a decade. But for many years I rolled with them each day while Cathlin was at work. I realize now how privileged we were to even have the choice for one of us to stay home with our children, but in the scrum of daily life, of often feeling as if my journey had ended rather than just begun, I didn't feel privileged; I felt sorry for myself.

On the phone, I listened to my friend unburden himself, something he very much needed to do. He was twenty years younger than I, in many ways a different generation. But he was also a peer because he was a parent, a time of life that transcends all age boundaries. We swapped stories about the hard times, the desperate times when all you want to do is escape the routine of eat, stroll, nap, cry, then cry some more. Once, in the sandbox when the kids were young, another stay-at-home dad smiled at me and said: "Don't we have the best job of all." I wanted to punch the guy, to apply a sleeper hold right there among the plastic buckets and Tonka trucks and toddlers learning to stand.

My friend and I laughed, and the laughter allowed us to go deeper.

I told him that when I was a new dad, in order to provide some much-needed cash to our bottom line, I started tutoring kids preparing for the SATs. This was back in New York City, and I still recall working with a student in the living room while his father paced, shirtless, periodically slapping his bare chest. I assumed the action was for my benefit, to remind me who was really in charge. Later, I learned that the father had recently been laid off from his finance job, and I saw more clearly the vision of another man unmoored like me from what he considered to be the natural order of things: going to an office and finding a community among the telephone calls and strategy sessions, the to-do lists and coffee banter.

The shirtless father frightened me, a version of myself I could see coming if I didn't stand watch over my insecurities and male ego. Then, at the last tutoring session, after I had shaken my student's hand and wished him good luck on that Saturday's test, the father followed me into the hallway. At the elevator door he extended his hand and as we shook— friendly, with no over-gripping—he said: "You'll never know how much you've given my son with your patience and thoughtfulness." I wanted to hug the man and tell him the same thing, that he'd never know how much his words meant to me. Instead, I ducked into the elevator, desperate to get away as quickly as I could.

I wish I had talked to that man, like I was talking to my friend, and shared my insecurities. That other father, I realized later, was teaching me something about vulnerability, how much we want for our children and how so often we can't measure up. Thankfully, life's road is filled with teachers and mentors, some clearly marked, others in disguise, bare-chested and hairy and lurking by the elevator.

The truth is, parenting is hard for everyone: dads, moms, grandparents, caregivers, the kids, too. There's no getting around that fact as we take on this role we have no real experience for. Which is why sharing stories from the trenches is important, bonding over the hard times as well as the good ones.

As my friend and I continued to talk, I switched direction and described to him places he had not yet visited: the far-off lands of middle school and high school. And then I told him about college essays, and how the boy who would never go to sleep at night was now a young man finding his voice.

I told him about caps and gowns, about my son walking across the stage to receive his high school diploma, and how my pride in his accomplishments was mirrored by my sadness that he would soon be leaving home.

I told my friend about passing my son's bedroom one afternoon and seeing it empty, then kneeling at the foot of my son's bed, bowing my head and inhaling the scent of his life. I told him about clinging to every single memory with the ferocity of a preschooler gripping the monkey bars, not wanting to leave the playground, not wanting to take a nap, not wanting to miss a single damn thing at all.

And I told him about that dad in the sandbox, and that he was right after all: It *is* the best job in the world.

49.

～～～

I DIDN'T CRY. I'M a crier, but I didn't cry when I prepared to drop Hardy off at college.

I didn't cry when we packed the car or drove onto the ferry. I didn't cry when we hit the highway—Hardy, Cathlin, Pickle, and me—heading south. I didn't cry then mostly because Hardy and Pickle were arguing in the backseat, and I was reminded of a drive many years ago when they were still young and arguing and annoying me. I pulled off the highway into a dingy gas station, told them to get out of the car, sat them down on a curb, and drove away. The incident quickly became the stuff of family legend: the time Dad left the kids on the side of the road (Cathlin, of course, was not with us that day). The story grew with each telling. I'd left them for hours, then for a whole day. In fact, it was only two minutes, and I didn't drive out of sight, just twenty yards or so.

I didn't cry because I was wondering about the young father I once was, so exhausted and confused that I would resort to scaring my children to get them to behave. Thankfully, Hardy and Pickle laugh about that memory now, like a family heirloom that's both good and bad.

I didn't cry when we pulled up to Hardy's dorm and un-packed the car. I didn't cry when we entered Hardy's room to unpack, or when I ran back downstairs to park the car so other parents could use the spot in front of the dorm.

I didn't cry after parking the car when I encountered an-other family saying goodbye, the college freshman hugging her little brother so hard she lifted him into the air, his small sneakers dangling as his body shook with tears. I almost cried when I saw the father, a burly man in cut-off sleeves with a huge tattoo circling his calf. He was leaning against their car, one arm outstretched for support while his body was folded in two and his tears spilled onto the sidewalk.

I *almost* cried then, but not quite.

I didn't even cry in the "Tunnel of Tears," a name Pickle gave to a small alcove that connected Hardy's dorm court-yard to the street. Parents lingered there after their final goodbye so their children wouldn't see them fully break down. Once out of sight, they rested their heads against a solid brick wall and let loose.

I *didn't* cry on the drive home, or when we pulled into the driveway and saw the house, listing, it seemed, as it prepared to welcome back three, not four. I didn't cry when we walked through the door and Artichoke rushed us, greeting us one by one, then paused and looked expectantly at the doorway for another person to walk in.

I didn't cry that night, while lying awake in bed recalling the Halloween when Hardy dressed as a lobster, the costume Cathlin made entirely from red Solo cups and plates. I didn't cry thinking about Legos, the Redwall books, picking up Hardy at preschool when every day for almost six months he made me sit at a small table in the hallway and feed him a maple yogurt and read *Animalia* to him while all the other parents headed to the playground.

I didn't cry when I remembered that after Cathlin's breast cancer diagnosis, when all we knew was fear, we sat down with Hardy because we wanted to be open with him about the hard road ahead. And seven-year-old Hardy looked at us and nodded, and then got out his crayons and filled a page with cancer villains, each one with a sinister mustache, and then slashed X's through them.

I didn't cry when I thought about laughing with him, cooking with him, asking him to stop reading me the news headlines each morning about the horrors of the world.

I didn't cry at any of these moments, and although I wondered why, I had no answers.

I didn't cry on the first morning home after we'd dropped him at college, when I woke, made my coffee, and walked downstairs to my writing room. I lit a candle and reached for my pencil and pad. But then I sensed a movement behind me and turned to look at the rocking chair in the corner and I imagined I saw Hardy there, at age six or seven. He didn't visit every morning but often enough, up early like me. He always brought a book with him and snuggled in the chair, reading quietly while I wrote.

When I finished writing and he put down his book, we would walk up the stairs together, ready to greet the day. I remembered walking up the stairs, Hardy's small hand in mine, knowing that whatever happened that day, all I had to do was recall that moment with my son and everything would be okay.

And that's when I began to cry.

50.

FAMILY LEGEND HAS it that Pickle's first word was *shoe*. By the time she was a teenager, the days of first words were a bit foggy, but that's the story Cathlin and I have always told ourselves. Looking at the vast collection of Pickle's shoes lining our living room when she was a freshman in high school, I could believe it.

In Pickle's defense, the shoes weren't all hers—we didn't have a mud room, so the family's shoes took center stage along one wall, stretching from the front door to the stereo—but the majority were: sneakers, sandals, clogs, more sneakers, boots, and more boots. I remember staring at the collection while waiting for her to finish getting ready for school. The morning routine was not as hectic since Hardy had left for college: roust just one child from bed, check on the day's scheduling, grab a piece of toast, and then wait at the door while calling out the countdown: *Four minutes and we have to be on the road. Two minutes or we'll be late. We're now officially late!*

When Hardy was born, Cathlin and I discovered that our gaze had narrowed as we focused intently on his every breath. But when Pickle arrived, three years later, we marveled at how the scope of our world seemed to enlarge; it was as if the horizon had returned as our attention shifted to two. There was less scrutiny within the chaos, which felt right. But when Hardy went away to college, the gaze shrank again. I noticed the way Pickle nibbled her fingernails, how she walked to the car with her backpack slung over one shoulder, how in the passenger seat she was no longer a little girl stretching to see over the dashboard.

Pickle's high school is a twenty-minute drive from our house, and she could have easily taken the bus—which she sometimes suggested on the mornings we followed behind the bus the entire way to school. But during her freshman year, I wasn't ready to give up those twenty minutes of traveling side by side, sometimes talking, sometimes quiet, sometimes listening to music. Without that routine, I didn't know how I would start my day.

ONE MORNING DRIVE, early in her freshman year, Pickle and I talked about Maybelle, our favorite chicken, who was dying.

Maybelle had become part of our lives eight years earlier when Pickle and Cynthia Riggs, a longtime islander and member of Cathlin's church, hatched a plan to convince me that backyard chickens were essential. I had never owned chickens, nor did I want to. But it was impossible to say no to the combined forces of a six-year-old and an octogenarian.

Pickle and Cynthia chose chicks from a mail-order catalog, and a few weeks later we picked them up at the post office and brought them home in a small box. Cathlin created a pen for them in the kitchen until they were old enough to be moved out to the backyard coop. There were seven chickens in that initial order and over the years the rest of the brood died, succumbing to either disease or hawks. Only Maybelle survived, making the rounds each day in the nearby woods, sometimes finding a safe place to hide at night when I forgot to close the coop door.

In her later years, Maybelle was surrounded by chickens we had inherited along the way, and some weren't nice to her. Thankfully, Janice befriended her and drove the other chickens away when they got too aggressive. Every day the twosome wandered off together, taking a circuitous path through the woods and roosting in the rhododendrons, where the thick leaves remained year-round, serving as a fortress against possible attacks from above.

Maybelle was always a mellow chicken, so calm that Pickle could take her to the ferry to greet friends. She also became the rocking-chair chicken. Most days she would fly up to the seat on our front porch and settle on the cushion to pass the time. Eventually, she began laying her eggs there rather than in the nesting box in the coop.

As she aged, she didn't have the strength to fly onto the rocker and I often found her resting beside it. Sometimes I picked her up and we sat together, Maybelle on my lap, as we looked out at the woods and thought our man and chicken thoughts.

WHEN PICKLE AND I arrived home the evening after our morning talk about Maybelle, the chicken looked especially tired, squatting close to the coop. We sat on the grass and fed her bits of banana, her favorite treat. Standing watch next to her was Janice. The banana seemed to revive Maybelle, and the two chickens strolled to the edge of the yard and scratched about in the leaves, looking for a final snack before bed.

Inside, Pickle went to her bedroom, while I headed for my room to gather my thoughts. But when I passed Hardy's room, I decided to go there instead. Hardy was now navigating his own freshman year, and the intimate journey of his everyday life, down to what he had eaten or how he looked when he first woke up, his hair disheveled as he reached for his glasses to check the time, was not part of my life anymore. Other dads had confided to me that when their child went off to college, they became troubled by the empty bedroom. Some kept the door closed all the time, others found themselves wandering in to straighten the bed covers or stare out the window for minutes at a time. I chose a different route, transferring several shirts of mine to Hardy's closet, claiming I had no more room in mine. It made visiting his room a potential daily occurrence, not a big or heavy thing.

"Just getting a shirt," I would tell Pickle or Cathlin when they found me in his room and asked why was there.

I looked out Hardy's window, which has the best view of the chicken coop. All the chickens were coming home to roost now as the day turned dark—Maybelle and Janice, too, walking slowly and side by side.

DRIVING TO SCHOOL the next day, Pickle and I talked about Maybelle some more. Eight years was old for a chicken, we acknowledged, and she had lived a good life. Then we fell silent, not knowing what else to say.

That evening we found Maybelle standing beneath the trampoline, looking weaker than ever, one eye open, the other closed. Even Janice looked worried.

Later, while putting the chickens to bed, we couldn't find Maybelle. We searched with flashlights until I heard a rustle near the porch rocker.

Maybelle's small head peeked out from a pile of leaves. She was tucked in for the night, barely visible, but I worried about the raccoons and carried her to the coop. She was too weak to hold on to her perch beside Janice, so I set her gently in a nesting box.

In the morning, I found Maybelle lying flat among the wood shavings. Both eyes were closed and I assumed she was dead. But when I touched her, she opened her eyes.

I got Pickle and together we moved Maybelle to a spot in the yard where she could be comfortable in her last moments and away from the other chickens, which had begun to peck at her, no matter how hard Janice tried to keep them away. The two of us watched Maybelle breathe. Then my attention shifted to Pickle. I saw her hand on Maybelle's back, stroking her feathers. I saw how long Pickle's fingers had grown, and how she used them to comfort Maybelle. I saw Pickle's clogs and her white sweatpants splattered with mud. I saw her shoulders begin to shake and I heard her sobs. I saw my own hand on Pickle's back—and then I saw, in my mind, my hand writing all of it down.

I have written about my children all their lives, have watched them and watched myself watching them. Occasionally, I've felt guilty about this as my father-self was swallowed up by my writer-self. But neither Hardy nor

Pickle ever asked me to stop sending stories of their private lives into the public sphere. It crossed my mind, though, while watching Pickle and Maybelle, that the day might soon come.

Sure enough, that night, after we had wrapped Maybelle in a towel and placed her in a box to bury her the next day, Pickle sent me a text from her bedroom.

"Please don't write about this," she texted.

"Okay," I texted back.

But the next morning, long before the sun rose, I put pencil to paper and wrote the story of Maybelle, even though I didn't think it would ever leave the basement. I had no other choice. It's how I paid attention to my life more deeply than I could in any other way. Putting words to our stories was how I told my children how much I loved them. And it was how I told them how much I missed them as they grew up and discovered lives of their own.

Later, as Pickle and I walked out the door to drive to school, Janice burst forth from the rhododendrons. She was alone and the sight clawed at my heart. I went back inside and gathered some Honey Nut Cheerios, a favorite treat of hers and Maybelle's, and sprinkled them on the lawn. As Janice pecked away, I told Pickle what I had written and asked her if it would be okay to share in the *Gazette*. I told her it was about Maybelle but so much more.

She thought for a moment.

"Okay," she said. "But this is the last time."

And with that she was off to the car, her backpack slung over her shoulder.

Pickle slid into the passenger seat, that middle ground between the car-seat days, when I snuck looks at her in the rear-view mirror, and the near future, when she'd take her place in the driver's seat.

And not long after that, I'd have to come up with another excuse, this time to visit her empty room, to straighten her pictures or to look out her window and wonder how her life was unfolding.

51.

⌇⌇⌇

A N EDITOR OF a national newspaper called to see if I
would be interested in writing a piece about summer on
Martha's Vineyard from a local's perspective.

"You know, like the coolest places to go, ways to score tickets, the hidden beaches, that sort of thing," the editor said.

"Well, beaches are easy," I said. "After all, we're an island:
all you have to do is drive until you see sand and water, then
park and jump in."

"No, I'm looking for the *inside* scoop. Do you have a
favorite?"

"Yes."

"Where all the celebrities and beautiful people go, right?"

"Actually, it's the one where my grandfather is buried."

"Excuse me?"

"It's near his favorite fishing hole. When he died, the
whole family went out in a flotilla of kayaks and we scattered
his ashes there."

"Recently?"

"No, many years ago."

"Kind of morbid. Any other beaches?"

"Well, there's one that frightens me."

"Big waves, right? Surfer spot?"

"Not exactly. It's where my brother and I were kidnapped when we were kids. We were hitchhiking and picked up by two men and a woman who wouldn't let us out. We kept asking, but they just kept driving. When they turned into a graveyard, my brother opened the door and we jumped out, hitting the dirt road and bouncing like a pair of skipping stones. We got away by running into the woods. The people were never caught."

"What are you trying to do, scare the tourists to Cape Cod?"

"Maybe."

"Next topic: restaurants. What was the last great meal you ate on the Vineyard."

"That's easy: roadkill venison tacos."

"Is that sort of thing legal at Vineyard restaurants?"

"It wasn't a restaurant. I was visiting my friend Chris. My son had to do an interview for the school newspaper. We went to visit Chris, who was opening up a new restaurant. He invited us to a lunch he was making for his grandmother and friends. While he cooked the roadkill venison on the grill, he also skinned a rabbit he'd shot that morning with a BB gun."

"Gross."

"Kind of. But delicious, too."

"Moving on. Any celebrities? Do you see Jake Gyllenhaal or Meg Ryan? How about Keith Richards? I hear he visits in the summer."

"No, not really. But I hang out a lot with Edward Hoagland."

"Never heard of him."

"He's one of the best nature essayists of the last half century."

"I'm falling asleep."

"Ted has written about almost every place on the planet but is blind now, so he mostly walks the streets of Edgartown, where he lives. We sit together during the afternoons on the porch of St. Andrew's Church, where he likes to rock in the sun. Last week he told me about Africa and the famines he witnessed there. He started crying while he remembered the horror of those days. Afterward, I walked him home, his hand on my outstretched arm so he wouldn't have to use his cane. He said he would write me a piece for the Gazette about walking, and this inspired me to take a walk of my own. I headed to the end of Fuller Street, to another beach I like, where I used to sit with my grandmother and eat egg sandwiches from the Dock Street Diner while looking out over the water. This was when she was dying and my wife and I moved here to take care of her. Sometimes we sat there for hours, just eating and looking, not talking much. She was cranky and funny. Once, the actor Fisher Stevens gave her two bottles of very good champagne because he didn't know how else to tell her how much he appreciated meeting her. We drank those bottles of champagne at the end of Fuller Street, pairing it with our egg sandwiches. My grandmother said it was her favorite meal ever."

"Finally, a celebrity story. But not what I had in mind. I can't even remember what Fisher Stevens was in."

"Lots of stuff, going way back to *The Flamingo Kid* and *Short Circuit*. A great character actor. You would recognize his voice."

"You know, there's a theme emerging here."

"What's that?"

"Old people and death."

"I guess you're right. Not what you're looking for, I imagine."

"No, not really."

"I have two children. Would that help?"

"Depends. What are they like?"

"Well, my daughter used to think she was a hobbit, even cut her hair once and taped it to the tops of her feet because hobbits have hairy feet. Then she was into Nancy Drew and spent a lot of time walking around with a magnifying glass and screwdriver saying she was working on the case of her adopted brother."

"Is your son adopted?"

"No. But he took the ribbing well enough. A few years ago, my daughter taped a note on the toilet that says, HARDY'S ROOM. So far he hasn't torn it off. And he and his friends are into making fun of me. They're really creative about it."

"For example?"

"He once created a T-shirt with my face on it and the words ALL PRAISE THE EYEBROWS."

"Do you have nice eyebrows?"

"No, not at all. Maybe when I was younger. It's tough to tell—that feels like so long ago. I just turned fifty-seven."

"What did you do for your birthday?"

"Drove my kids around to their activities . . . baseball and dance, that sort of thing. Hugged my wife. And then, later that night, I sat alone on the porch and listened to my life."

"You know, I really don't think you're the writer for this piece. I had something very different in mind."

"I agree. I'm not the writer for the piece you had in mind."

"But it was nice talking to you. By the way, when you were sitting on the porch, what did you hear?"

"The crickets chirping, a woman laughing, a dog barking, the wind whispering. The grass and the stars joined in, too, as they always do."

"And what did it all sound like?"

"Home. It sounded like home."

EPILOGUE

I T'S SUNDAY MORNING and Pickle and I decide to drive Hardy's car to church. The muffler is broken, so our arrival is announced by a mighty roar. I'll need to make an appointment to get it fixed before Hardy comes home for his holiday break from college. But for now, I enjoy my excursions in his tumble-down beater of an island car. In addition to the muffler problem, one door is a different color—a junkyard replacement after a minor collision—and the hood doesn't fully close. I feel like I'm in disguise when I drive Hardy's car, a young kid again cruising in his first ride. But mostly I like driving Hardy's car because it reminds me of him, his baseball cleats still in the backseat, along with a book on Bruegel's paintings, a necklace hanging from the rear-view mirror—in these moments he's back with us, Pickle, Hardy, and I racing out the door to make it to church on time.

Cathlin left the house hours earlier to get the church ready and orient herself to the mood of the morning. When Pickle and I arrive, we settle into our pew: right side, seven rows back. At some point over the years our seating shifted a few rows. I don't remember when or why this happened, but where we sit now feels right.

The congregation has gradually increased again in the last few months as coronavirus fears have eased. Some still choose to attend by Zoom, making Sundays in church a hybrid event. Their faces are projected on the walls on both sides of the pulpit. During the service, Cathlin will have us all wave to those attending from their homes. In the pews, much of what we see is the backs of heads, but the Zoomers look out at us and we at them, making the moment feel like a call to grandma or a cousin we haven't seen in a while. It is oddly comforting.

As more people trickle in, the organist plays a prelude and I look around, noticing new faces and absent ones. Chuck and Martha died last year, and I miss them both—Martha and her daffodil tours each spring and Chuck with his hearty hello and what he referred to as "the Galápagos Grip," where instead of simply shaking my hand he'd clasp my forearm and ask me to do the same. "It's how you hoist someone out of the lifeboat," he told me. "I learned that on a tour of the Galápagos."

But Steve is here: left side, third row. Steve is a retired creative writing professor who recently moved to the Vineyard. I had immediately asked him to write an essay for the Gazette, and when he sent me one about his love of reading the obituaries, I knew we'd be good friends.

I turn to Pickle and ask her to pass me the pencil at the edge of the pew on top of the welcome pad for newcomers to write their contact information. She gives me a look, knowing this means I'm thinking about an essay I want to write and need to jot down some details.

"Not about me," she says as she hands me the pencil.

"Of course not," I reply, remembering the early days when we would draw together in the pew. Now she's a teenager, and I can tell she's here and not here, just like I was as a teenager in church, putting in the time but itching to get on with my day.

I hear a siren, the sound rising as it gets closer to the church and then fading as the police car races away. I wonder what's going on, an accident, someone speeding, or maybe a lead in the armed bank robbery that took place earlier in the week. A bank robbery is a rare thing for the Vineyard. In the newsroom, we researched when the last one had taken place—it was in 1987 and involved a bow and arrow and money stashed in someone's wooden leg.

After church I'll head to the newsroom and make some calls, checking in with the police and the reporters. Recently, I was made editor of the *Vineyard Gazette*, a twist in my story I didn't see coming, though when it arrived felt inevitable. I remember a writing teacher once telling me that good stories have a trajectory: when they end there should first be a feeling of surprise at the turn of events, but then, after looking back at the breadcrumbs, a sense that, *Of course, that's where this tale was always headed!* After all, the *Vineyard Gazette* and I share the same birthday: May 14.

But for now I settle in as Cathlin steps to the pulpit and addresses the congregation. She is confident but humble, joyous but grounded as she greets everyone and asks us to pass the peace. The congregation erupts into conversation, waving and talking and shaking hands, the community of the faithful checking in with one another as they do every Sunday. Once again I'm amazed at the energy and happy that I'm here.

When the congregation has quieted down, Cathlin goes over the announcements, talking about the prayer groups meeting during the week, preparations for the holiday fair and the Christmas pageant coming up. Then we stand and sing together, our voices ringing out as one in the old church as they have for more than three hundred years.

When it's time for the children's message, only a few kids walk to the front pew. Many families have not yet returned to the rhythms of church life since the worst days of the pandemic, so I nudge Pickle to see if she'll join the children, but she shakes her head. Then Dorothy, a woman nearing ninety, rises. "I'm a kid at heart," she announces and walks up front. The congregation laughs and applauds.

After the message for the children, Cathlin settles into her sermon. I listen, as I always do, as her husband and her editor. But more and more, I've come to discover, I listen as her congregant, hungry for her message.

It is Gratitude Sunday, Cathlin begins. As the sermon progresses and deepens, she takes us on a journey of not only giving thanks but also of honoring those who have come before us and those who will travel in our footsteps. We do that, she says, by remembering the burdens they carried and have yet to carry. We honor each other by sharing not only our joys but our sorrows, too.

Cathlin often talks about the Celtic phrase caol áit, which translates to "thin places," those moments and places where the distance between the world of the spirits and the world of the flesh vanishes. It is in the presence of "thin places" that we feel most connected to the ghosts who have accompanied us on our journey and are a part of the stories we tell.

Martha's Vineyard is a "thin place" for me. At every bend in the road, I encounter the deep past of my ancestors who arrived long ago, but I also see clearly my recent past. We moved here fourteen years ago, raised our children, and watched Hardy leave to begin the next chapter of his life—we'll soon watch Pickle do the same. And all along the way I've felt accompanied by both this thriving, living community and the community I visit when I walk Artichoke through the island's many graveyards.

Church has also become a "thin place" for me, a front-row seat to witness the complexities of living where the past sits just a pew away. I can see myself seated in our old pew, holding Pickle in my arms as she turns to look up at the choir loft, her pudgy one-year-old face aglow. I see Hardy bent over a piece of paper, drawing a detailed parting of the Red Sea. I see Cathlin standing at the pulpit, bald save a single hair that no one but her family could see. I see myself walking into the Gazette on my first day, nervous about starting all over again. I see myself trying hard to become the man I always wanted to be, inching closer and closer here on this island out at sea.

When the service ends, Pickle and I walk through the receiving line and I shake Cathlin's hand like the rest of the congregation. This feels both odd and comfortable, a moment to acknowledge that Cathlin is, in a way, both my wife and my pastor. I am a minister's husband, and I'm proud of this. When I introduce myself in this way, I no longer make excuses. It is who I am and how I navigate the world. It's a gift, I've come to understand, and one I acknowledge here on Gratitude Sunday.

As I mingle at coffee hour, Pickle tells me she is heading off to meet a friend. I say goodbye and watch her walk down the street. Then I find Cathlin and together we make our own way out into the world, once again ready for the real service to begin.

ACKNOWLEDGMENTS

With thanks to anyone who ever gave me encouragement and said *Yes*, and to my children who did not say *No*, until the very end.

———————————

A version of chapter 9 appeared as "The Hitcher" on *This American Life* on October 27, 2006.

A version of chapter 21 appeared as "Why He Moved into My Car, and Why I Let Him" in the *New York Times* on November 25, 2007.

A version of chapter 43 appeared as "As He Cut My Hair, I Wept" in the *New York Times* column Modern Love on June 26, 2020.

Portions of this book originally appeared as essays in the *Vineyard Gazette*.

A NOTE ABOUT THE AUTHOR

Bill Eville is the editor of the *Vineyard Gazette*. He grew up in New Jersey. After earning a degree in economics from Princeton University, he moved to New York City, where he lived for twenty years. He worked in banking and the film industry before moving with his wife and two children to Martha's Vineyard, where his ancestors landed as whalers in the early 1700s. Eville's writing has been featured in the *New York Times*, *This American Life*, *The Moth*, WBUR's *Cognoscenti*, and many other publications.

A NOTE ON THE TYPE

Washed Ashore has been set in Matthew Carter's Miller, a family of types derived from the roman letterforms designed in Scotland during the first decades of the nineteenth century, which becoming widely popular in the United States as general-purpose types for book and jobbing work. Miller, first released in 1997, was designed to be faithful to its antecedents without being a rote copy of any single source. Berthold Wolpe's Albertus has been used for the chapter numerals.

Design & Composition by Tammy Ackerman